J. CHAMBERS

The Cashless Revolution

How Gen Alpha and Gen Z are Transforming Payments

Copyright © 2024 by J. Chambers

All rights reserved. No part of this publication may be reproduced, stored or transmitted in any form or by any means, electronic, mechanical, photocopying, recording, scanning, or otherwise without written permission from the publisher. It is illegal to copy this book, post it to a website, or distribute it by any other means without permission.

J. Chambers asserts the moral right to be identified as the author of this work.

J. Chambers has no responsibility for the persistence or accuracy of URLs for external or third-party Internet Websites referred to in this publication and does not guarantee that any content on such Websites is, or will remain, accurate or appropriate.

Designations used by companies to distinguish their products are often claimed as trademarks. All brand names and product names used in this book and on its cover are trade names, service marks, trademarks and registered trademarks of their respective owners. The publishers and the book are not associated with any product or vendor mentioned in this book. None of the companies referenced within the book have endorsed the book.

First edition

This book was professionally typeset on Reedsy.
Find out more at reedsy.com

Contents

1	Chapter 1	1
2	Chapter 2	13
3	Chapter 3	28
4	Chapter 4	43
5	Chapter 5	61
6	Chapter 6	76
7	Chapter 7	89
8	Chapter 8	109
9	Chapter 9	125
10	Chapter 10	140
11	Chapter 11	155
12	Chapter 12	169
13	Chapter 13	173

1

Chapter 1

The advent of digital wallets and payment apps marks a significant transformation in the way people manage their finances, conduct transactions, and engage with financial services. The rise of these technologies has been especially pronounced among younger generations, namely Gen Alpha and Gen Z, who have grown up in a world where digital interactions are the norm. This shift toward digital financial tools is reshaping the financial landscape and setting the stage for a future where cashless transactions could become the global standard.

Digital wallets, also known as e-wallets, are software-based systems that securely store users' payment information and passwords for numerous payment methods and websites. Examples include Apple Pay, Google Wallet, and Samsung Pay. These wallets enable users to complete transactions quickly and conveniently, often with just a tap or scan. Payment apps like Venmo, Cash App, and PayPal extend this functionality by allowing peer-to-peer (P2P) transfers, bill payments, and even direct deposit capabilities. The convenience, speed, and security offered by these digital tools are major factors driving their adoption.

One of the key reasons for the rise of digital wallets and payment apps is the rapid advancement in mobile technology. Smartphones have become ubiquitous, with capabilities that extend far beyond simple communication. They serve as mini-computers, offering internet access, high-quality cameras, GPS, and more. The integration of payment functionalities into these devices is a natural progression, transforming them into powerful tools for managing personal finances. This seamless integration appeals particularly to younger generations, who are digital natives.

Gen Alpha and Gen Z have unique financial behaviors and preferences that make them prime adopters of digital wallets and payment apps. These generations value convenience, speed, and security. They are accustomed to instant gratification and seamless digital experiences, thanks to their upbringing in the age of the internet and smartphones. Traditional banking methods, which often involve physical visits to banks, long processing times, and cumbersome paperwork, seem outdated and inefficient to them.

Social media also plays a significant role in promoting digital wallets and payment apps among younger users. Platforms like Instagram, TikTok, and Snapchat are not just channels for social interaction but also spaces for financial education and promotion. Influencers and financial educators use these platforms to share tips on budgeting, saving, and using financial tools, making the concept of digital finance more accessible and appealing. Viral trends and peer influence further accelerate the adoption of these technologies.

Security and privacy, often concerns in the realm of digital transactions, are addressed robustly by digital wallets and payment apps. These platforms employ advanced encryption methods, tokenization, and biometric authentication (like fingerprint and facial recognition) to protect users' data and transactions. Despite occasional high-profile breaches, the overall security measures are strong, and young users often perceive digital wallets as safer than carrying cash or using traditional credit cards, which can be lost or stolen.

Financial literacy is another critical aspect where digital wallets and payment apps are making a positive impact. Many of these platforms offer features that help users manage their money more effectively. For example, budgeting tools, spending trackers, and notifications about upcoming bills or low balances are commonly integrated into these apps. This real-time access to financial information helps Gen Alpha and Gen Z develop better financial habits early on. Moreover, the gamification of finance, where users earn rewards or badges for certain financial behaviors, makes learning about money management more engaging.

The future of cashless transactions looks promising, with digital wallets and payment apps at the forefront. The trend towards a cashless society is driven by the convenience and efficiency that these tools provide. As more retailers and service providers accept digital payments, the necessity for physical cash diminishes. In some countries, like Sweden, the move towards a cashless economy is already well underway, with a significant portion of transactions conducted electronically.

However, the transition to a fully cashless society is not without challenges. Digital wallets and payment apps rely heavily on internet access and digital literacy, which are not uniformly available across all demographics and regions. Ensuring that the benefits of digital finance are accessible to everyone, including the unbanked and underbanked populations, is a significant hurdle. Additionally, there are concerns about data privacy and the potential for financial exclusion of those who are less tech-savvy.

Globally, the adoption of digital wallets and payment apps varies. In Asia, particularly in countries like China and India, mobile payments are extremely popular, driven by platforms like Alipay, WeChat Pay, and Paytm. These platforms offer a wide range of services beyond payments, including social networking, e-commerce, and even investment opportunities, making them integral to daily life. In contrast, the adoption rate in some Western countries has been slower, but it is accelerating as consumers become more comfortable with digital transactions and as more merchants accept these payment methods.

The rise of digital wallets and payment apps is not just a trend; it represents a fundamental shift in the way we think about money and transactions. For Gen Alpha and Gen Z, these technologies are not just convenient tools but integral parts of their financial lives. As they mature and their financial needs grow, the features and functionalities of digital wallets and payment apps are likely to evolve, offering even more sophisticated services.

In conclusion, the growth of digital wallets and payment apps marks a significant milestone in the evolution of financial technology. Driven by advancements in mobile technology, the influence of social media, and the unique preferences of younger generations, these tools are redefining how we manage money. While challenges remain, particularly in terms of accessibility and security, the future of cashless transactions looks bright, with digital wallets and payment apps leading the way. As Gen Alpha and Gen Z continue to embrace these technologies, we can expect a more connected, efficient, and secure financial ecosystem.

Generation Alpha and Generation Z represent the newest cohorts of digital natives, born into a world deeply entrenched in technology and connectivity. As the first generations to grow up with smartphones, social media, and ubiquitous internet access from a very young age, their behaviors, values, and expectations are markedly different from those of previous generations. Understanding these generations is crucial for businesses, educators, policymakers, and anyone interested in the future landscape of society and commerce.

Generation Z (Gen Z) encompasses individuals born roughly between 1997 and 2012. This generation follows Millennials and is currently entering adulthood and the workforce. They are characterized by their deep familiarity with technology and digital environments. Gen Z's formative years were shaped by the rapid advancement of mobile technology, the rise of social media, and significant global events such as the financial crisis of 2008 and the COVID-19 pandemic. These experiences have influenced their values, financial behaviors, and perspectives on the world.

Gen Z is often described as the most diverse generation in history, with a strong emphasis on inclusivity and social justice. They tend to be pragmatic, financially cautious, and value experiences over material possessions. Financially, Gen Z is more conservative than Millennials, having witnessed the economic challenges faced by their predecessors. They prioritize saving, are skeptical of debt, and are more likely to use financial apps and digital wallets to manage their money.

Digital literacy is a hallmark of Gen Z. They are comfortable navigating multiple devices and platforms, often multitasking across several at once. This digital fluency extends to their financial behaviors, where they expect seamless, intuitive, and mobile-first financial services. Gen Z's reliance on technology influences their shopping habits as well, with a strong preference for online shopping and digital payment methods. They are also influenced heavily by social media, not just for social interactions but for making purchasing decisions and financial choices.

Generation Alpha (Gen Alpha) refers to those born from 2013 onwards, following Gen Z. While they are still children and early adolescents, their early years are marked by an even deeper integration with technology. Gen Alpha is growing up with voice assistants, smart devices, and highly interactive digital content. By the time they reach adulthood, the digital landscape will have evolved further, shaping their behaviors and expectations in ways we are only beginning to understand.

Gen Alpha is set to be the most educated generation, with education systems increasingly integrating digital tools and personalized learning experiences. They are expected to be even more comfortable with technology than Gen Z, given their exposure from birth. This constant interaction with technology is likely to make them highly adept at using digital tools for education, entertainment, and eventually, financial management.

The financial behaviors of Gen Alpha will be shaped by the precedents set by Gen Z and the continuing evolution of financial technologies. Digital wallets, payment apps, and potentially new innovations like digital currencies will be integral to their financial interactions. Gen Alpha will expect hyper-personalized and seamless financial services, with a strong emphasis on security and ease of use.

The Role of Technology in Shaping Gen Z and Gen Alpha

Both generations are defined by their interactions with technology. For Gen Z, the proliferation of smartphones and social media during their formative years created a unique environment where they could communicate, learn, and shop online. This generation witnessed the rise of influencers and the power of viral content, which significantly impacts their consumer behavior and brand loyalty.

Gen Z's financial habits are also influenced by technology. They are more likely to use budgeting apps, digital wallets, and investment platforms tailored to novice investors. This generation values financial education and seeks out information from digital sources, including social media, where financial influencers offer advice and tips.

For Gen Alpha, technology is even more embedded in their daily lives. They are growing up with artificial intelligence, smart home devices, and highly interactive educational tools. This constant exposure will likely result in an unparalleled comfort with technology and a preference for digital solutions in all aspects of life, including finance.

As Gen Alpha matures, they will benefit from advancements in financial technology that are just emerging today. This includes greater use of blockchain, artificial intelligence in financial planning, and potentially widespread use of digital currencies. The expectation of seamless, instant, and secure financial transactions will be even more pronounced in Gen Alpha than in Gen Z.

Social and Cultural Influences

Gen Z and Gen Alpha are also shaped by significant social and cultural trends. Gen Z is known for its strong advocacy for social justice, environmental sustainability, and diversity. They value authenticity and are quick to support brands and companies that align with their values. This generation is also more likely to be involved in activism and use their purchasing power to support ethical and sustainable practices.

For Gen Alpha, social and cultural influences will continue to evolve. They are growing up in a time when discussions about climate change, social justice, and global interconnectedness are at the forefront. These influences will shape their worldviews and potentially make them even more conscientious consumers than Gen Z.

Implications for Businesses and Financial Institutions

Understanding the behaviors and expectations of Gen Z and Gen Alpha is crucial for businesses and financial institutions. These generations will drive demand for digital-first services that are intuitive, secure, and aligned with their values. Companies that can offer seamless digital experiences, prioritize security, and engage with these generations authentically will be well-positioned for success.

Financial institutions, in particular, need to adapt to the digital preferences of these generations. This includes offering robust mobile banking options, integrating AI for personalized financial advice, and ensuring top-notch cybersecurity measures. Additionally, financial education will be key, as both generations value understanding their financial options and making informed decisions.

CHAPTER 1

The Importance of Studying the Financial Behaviors of Gen Alpha and Gen Z

In a rapidly evolving financial landscape, understanding the financial behaviors of Generation Alpha (Gen Alpha) and Generation Z (Gen Z) is crucial for a myriad of stakeholders, including businesses, financial institutions, policymakers, and educators. These generations, born into a world of advanced technology and unprecedented connectivity, are shaping the future of finance in ways that are both profound and transformative. Studying their financial behaviors not only provides insights into current trends but also helps anticipate future changes in the financial ecosystem.

Technological Integration and Digital Fluency

One of the defining characteristics of Gen Alpha and Gen Z is their deep integration with technology. Gen Z, born between 1997 and 2012, and Gen Alpha, born from 2013 onwards, are digital natives. They have grown up with smartphones, tablets, and the internet, making them exceptionally comfortable with digital tools and platforms. This digital fluency extends to their financial behaviors, where they favor digital wallets, payment apps, and online banking over traditional banking methods.

Understanding how these generations interact with digital financial tools is vital for businesses and financial institutions. For example, the preference for mobile banking and digital wallets such as Venmo, Cash App, and Apple Pay indicates a shift away from cash and traditional banking methods. This trend underscores the need for financial institutions to invest in digital infrastructure and enhance their mobile offerings to cater to the needs of these tech-savvy consumers.

Economic Impacts and Spending Habits

Gen Z and Gen Alpha are poised to become major economic drivers in the coming decades. According to a report by Bank of America, Gen Z alone will account for a quarter of global income by 2030. Their spending habits, therefore, will have significant implications for the economy. Gen Z is characterized by a pragmatic and cautious approach to money, likely influenced by witnessing the financial struggles of previous generations during the Great Recession.

Studying the spending habits of these generations helps businesses tailor their products and marketing strategies. For instance, Gen Z tends to prioritize experiences over material possessions, leading to a rise in the experiential economy. This generation is also known for valuing sustainability and ethical consumption, which influences their purchasing decisions. Companies that align their values with those of Gen Z, such as through sustainable practices and ethical sourcing, are more likely to capture their loyalty.

Financial Literacy and Education

Financial literacy is a critical area of focus for Gen Alpha and Gen Z. Despite their comfort with digital tools, there is a notable gap in financial literacy among these generations. According to a report by the National Endowment for Financial Education (NEFE), only 24% of Gen Z demonstrate basic financial literacy. This gap presents both a challenge and an opportunity for educators and policymakers.

Promoting financial literacy among these generations is crucial for their financial well-being and for the broader economy. Financially literate individuals are better equipped to make informed decisions about saving, investing, and managing debt. Educational initiatives, both in schools and through digital platforms, can help bridge this gap. Financial institutions also have a role to play by providing resources and tools that promote financial education.

Investment Behaviors and Trends

Gen Z and, eventually, Gen Alpha are reshaping the investment landscape. Unlike previous generations, they have access to a plethora of online investment platforms and resources. This democratization of investing has led to increased participation in the stock market and other investment avenues. Platforms like Robinhood and Acorns have made investing accessible to younger generations by lowering the barriers to entry.

Studying the investment behaviors of these generations reveals a trend towards socially responsible investing (SRI). Gen Z, in particular, shows a strong preference for investments that align with their values, such as environmental sustainability and social justice. This shift is influencing the financial markets, with a growing number of investment products catering to the demand for SRI.

Impact of Social Media and Influencers

Social media plays a pivotal role in shaping the financial behaviors of Gen Alpha and Gen Z. Platforms like Instagram, TikTok, and YouTube are not just social networking sites but also sources of financial education and influence. Financial influencers, or "finfluencers," share advice on budgeting, saving, investing, and using financial tools. Their content can reach millions of young viewers, significantly impacting their financial behaviors and decisions.

Understanding the influence of social media is essential for financial institutions and educators. Collaborating with trusted influencers can be an effective way to reach these generations and promote financial literacy. Moreover, monitoring trends on social media can provide insights into emerging financial behaviors and preferences, allowing institutions to adapt their strategies accordingly.

Challenges and Opportunities

While studying the financial behaviors of Gen Alpha and Gen Z presents numerous opportunities, it also comes with challenges. One significant challenge is the rapid pace of technological change, which can make it difficult to keep up with the latest trends and tools favored by these generations. Additionally, there is a risk of digital exclusion for those who lack access to technology or the skills to use it effectively.

Despite these challenges, there are substantial opportunities for businesses and financial institutions. By understanding the preferences and behaviors of these generations, companies can develop products and services that meet their needs. For example, offering personalized financial advice through AI-driven tools can appeal to Gen Z's desire for customized solutions. Similarly, gamifying financial education can make learning about money management more engaging for Gen Alpha.

The Future of Financial Services

The financial behaviors of Gen Alpha and Gen Z are setting the stage for the future of financial services. These generations expect seamless, intuitive, and instant financial interactions. They value transparency, security, and ethical practices. As they become the dominant consumer groups, their preferences will drive innovation and transformation in the financial sector.

Financial institutions need to be proactive in responding to these trends. Investing in digital infrastructure, enhancing cybersecurity measures, and promoting financial literacy are essential steps. Additionally, embracing the values of sustainability and social responsibility can help build trust and loyalty among these generations.

Chapter 2

Understanding Digital Wallets and Payment Apps

In today's digital age, **digital wallets** and **payment apps** have revolutionized the way we handle financial transactions. These tools offer convenience, speed, and security, transforming everything from how we shop to how we transfer money. Understanding the various types of digital wallets and payment apps, along with their functionalities, is essential for navigating the modern financial landscape.

Definition of Digital Wallets and Payment Apps

Digital wallets, also known as **e-wallets**, are electronic devices or online services that allow individuals to make electronic transactions. This can include purchasing items online or in-store, transferring money to others, and storing various forms of digital currency. A digital wallet securely stores users' payment information and passwords, enabling them to pay using their devices without the need for physical cards or cash.

Payment apps are mobile applications that facilitate the transfer of money between parties. These apps often integrate with digital wallets to allow for a range of financial activities, from peer-to-peer (P2P) payments to bill payments and even investment options. They are designed to be user-friendly and provide a seamless transaction experience.

Types of Digital Wallets

Digital wallets come in several forms, each catering to different needs and offering unique functionalities.

1. **Closed Wallets Closed wallets** are specific to a particular company and can only be used to transact with that company. For example, the **Starbucks app** allows users to store funds and make purchases exclusively at Starbucks locations. These wallets are often linked to loyalty programs, providing incentives for repeated use.
2. **Semi-Closed Wallets Semi-closed wallets** can be used at multiple locations, but they are limited to a specific list of merchants or vendors that have agreements with the wallet provider. **Paytm** in India is an example, where users can pay for services and goods at partner outlets.
3. **Open Wallets Open wallets** can be used for a wide range of transactions and are often issued by banks or institutions in collaboration with financial service providers. These wallets allow for withdrawal of funds from ATMs, online transactions, and payments at any accepting merchant. **PayPal**, **Google Wallet**, and **Apple Pay** are examples of open wallets.
4. **Cryptocurrency Wallets Cryptocurrency wallets** are digital wallets that store cryptocurrencies such as Bitcoin, Ethereum, and others. These wallets manage the cryptographic keys associated with digital currencies, enabling

users to send and receive crypto. **Coinbase** and **Ledger** are popular cryptocurrency wallets.

Types of Payment Apps

Payment apps also come in various forms, each designed to facilitate specific types of transactions.

1. **Peer-to-Peer (P2P) Payment Apps P2P payment apps** allow users to transfer money directly to others using their mobile devices. These apps are highly popular for their convenience and speed. Examples include **Venmo**, **Cash App**, and **Zelle**. They are often used for splitting bills, paying friends, and transferring money to family members.
2. **Mobile Payment Apps Mobile payment apps** facilitate in-store and online payments through mobile devices. **Apple Pay, Google Pay,** and **Samsung Pay** are leading mobile payment apps that allow users to make purchases by tapping their phones at point-of-sale terminals or using their devices online.
3. **Banking Apps Banking apps** are provided by traditional banks and offer a range of services including balance checks, fund transfers, bill payments, and mobile deposits. Apps like **Chase Mobile, Wells Fargo Mobile,** and **Bank of America Mobile Banking** fall into this category.
4. **Retailer-Specific Apps Retailer-specific apps** are developed by individual retailers to enhance the shopping experience by integrating payment options, loyalty programs, and personalized offers. The **Amazon app** and **Walmart Pay** are examples where users can store payment methods and complete purchases within the app.
5. **Cryptocurrency Payment Apps Cryptocurrency payment**

apps enable users to make transactions using their digital currency holdings. These apps often support multiple cryptocurrencies and integrate with digital wallets to facilitate purchases and transfers. **BitPay** and **Crypto.com** are examples.

Advantages of Digital Wallets and Payment Apps

The benefits of digital wallets and payment apps are numerous, driving their widespread adoption.

Convenience: One of the primary benefits of digital wallets and payment apps is the convenience they offer. Users can make payments, transfer money, and manage their finances from their smartphones without needing to carry physical cash or cards.

Speed: Transactions using digital wallets and payment apps are often faster than traditional methods. Instant transfers and quick payments enhance the user experience and are especially beneficial for busy lifestyles.

Security: Digital wallets and payment apps offer robust security features, including encryption, biometric authentication (such as fingerprint or facial recognition), and two-factor authentication. These measures help protect users' financial information and reduce the risk of fraud.

Integration with Loyalty Programs: Many digital wallets and payment apps integrate with loyalty programs, providing users with rewards, discounts, and special offers. This integration encourages repeated use and enhances customer engagement.

Global Reach: Digital wallets and payment apps can be used internationally, making them ideal for travelers and those conducting business across borders. This global reach eliminates the need for currency exchange and simplifies international transactions.

Disadvantages and Challenges

While digital wallets and payment apps offer many advantages, they are not without challenges.

Digital Divide: Access to digital wallets and payment apps requires a smartphone and internet connectivity, which may not be available to everyone, especially in rural or underserved areas. This digital divide can exclude certain populations from the benefits of digital finance.

Security Concerns: While digital wallets and payment apps offer enhanced security, they are not immune to cyber threats. Phishing attacks, data breaches, and other cybercrimes can compromise users' financial information. Continuous vigilance and security updates are necessary to mitigate these risks.

Dependency on Technology: Overreliance on digital wallets and payment apps can pose a problem if technical issues arise. System outages, software bugs, or device malfunctions can disrupt access to funds and transactions.

Regulatory and Compliance Issues: The regulatory environment for digital wallets and payment apps varies by country. Compliance with different regulations can be challenging for providers operating internationally, and changes in regulations can impact service offerings.

Future Trends

The future of digital wallets and payment apps is promising, with several trends indicating continued growth and innovation:

1. **Integration with Emerging Technologies:** Integration with **blockchain, artificial intelligence (AI)**, and **Internet of Things (IoT)** is expected to enhance the functionalities of digital wallets and payment apps. These technologies

can improve security, personalization, and transaction efficiency.
2. **Expansion of Contactless Payments:** The trend towards **contactless payments** is likely to continue, driven by consumer preferences for hygiene and convenience. More merchants will adopt contactless payment terminals, and digital wallets will enhance support for this technology.
3. **Growth in Cryptocurrency Adoption:** As cryptocurrencies gain wider acceptance, cryptocurrency wallets and payment apps will become more mainstream. Businesses and consumers will increasingly use digital currencies for transactions.
4. **Enhanced Financial Inclusion:** Digital wallets and payment apps have the potential to improve financial inclusion by providing access to financial services for unbanked and underbanked populations. Innovations targeting these groups can help bridge the financial divide.
5. **Personalized Financial Services:** Advances in AI and data analytics will enable digital wallets and payment apps to offer more personalized financial services, such as tailored budgeting advice, spending insights, and customized investment recommendations.

Historical Context and Evolution of Digital Payment Systems

The history of **digital payment systems** is a fascinating journey of innovation and technological advancement. From the early days of barter systems to the modern digital wallets and payment apps, the methods of exchanging value have evolved significantly. This evolution has been driven by the need for convenience, security, and efficiency in transactions. Understanding the historical context and the various milestones in the development of digital payment systems provides valuable insights into the future of financial transactions.

The Early Days: Barter and Coinage

Before the advent of formalized currency, people relied on barter systems to trade goods and services. The limitations of barter, such as the need for a double coincidence of wants, led to the development of money. The first known coins date back to ancient Lydia (modern-day Turkey) around 600 BCE. Coinage provided a standardized medium of exchange, making transactions simpler and more efficient.

The Introduction of Paper Money

The next significant evolution in payment systems came with the introduction of paper money. The earliest recorded use of paper money was in China during the Tang Dynasty (618-907 CE), but it became more widespread during the Song Dynasty (960-1279 CE). Paper money was lighter and easier to carry than metal coins, facilitating trade over longer distances.

The Rise of Banking and Checks

With the rise of banking institutions in medieval Europe, new payment methods began to emerge. By the 17th century, checks had become a common means of payment, allowing individuals to transfer money without carrying large sums of cash. The use of checks provided a safer and more convenient way to handle large transactions.

The Advent of Electronic Payments

The 20th century saw the introduction of electronic payment systems, beginning with wire transfers. Western Union launched the first widely used electronic fund transfer (EFT) system in 1871, enabling telegraphic money transfers. This system laid the groundwork for future electronic payment innovations.

The Credit Card Revolution

The introduction of the credit card in the 1950s marked a significant milestone in the evolution of payment systems. Diners Club issued the first universal credit card in 1950, followed by American Express in 1958. Credit cards allowed consumers to make purchases on credit and pay later, revolutionizing consumer spending and financial transactions.

The Emergence of Online Banking

The rise of the internet in the 1990s paved the way for online banking. Banks began offering online services, allowing customers to manage their accounts, transfer money, and pay bills through the internet. This shift provided unprecedented convenience and accessibility, transforming the way people handled their finances.

The Birth of Digital Wallets

The concept of **digital wallets** emerged in the late 1990s and early 2000s with the advent of e-commerce. PayPal, founded in 1998, was one of the first digital wallets, enabling secure online payments. Digital wallets store payment information and facilitate online transactions without the need for physical cards. This innovation significantly boosted the growth of e-commerce by providing a secure and convenient payment method.

Mobile Payments and NFC Technology

The proliferation of smartphones in the 2010s led to the development of **mobile payment** systems. Companies like Apple, Google, and Samsung introduced mobile wallets that use **near-field communication (NFC)** technology. **Apple Pay**, launched in 2014, allows users to make payments by tapping their phones at contactless terminals. **Google Wallet** (now Google Pay) and

Samsung Pay followed suit, integrating mobile payments into the everyday consumer experience.

Peer-to-Peer (P2P) Payment Systems

The rise of P2P payment systems further revolutionized the way people transfer money. Services like **Venmo**, **Cash App**, and **Zelle** enable users to send and receive money instantly using their smartphones. These apps provide a convenient alternative to traditional banking transfers, especially for smaller transactions and splitting bills among friends.

Cryptocurrencies and Blockchain Technology

The introduction of **Bitcoin** in 2009 by an anonymous entity known as **Satoshi Nakamoto** marked the beginning of a new era in digital payments. Bitcoin is a decentralized digital currency based on **blockchain technology**, which ensures secure and transparent transactions without the need for intermediaries. The success of Bitcoin paved the way for the development of thousands of other cryptocurrencies and blockchain-based payment systems. Cryptocurrencies offer an alternative to traditional financial systems, with the potential for lower transaction fees and increased privacy.

The Evolution of Payment Apps

The evolution of digital payment systems continued with the development of versatile **payment apps**. These apps integrate various financial services, including mobile banking, P2P payments, and digital wallets. Examples include **Alipay** and **WeChat Pay** in China, which have become ubiquitous in the region. These apps offer a wide range of services beyond payments, such as shopping, booking services, and even investing, making them integral to daily life.

Contactless Payments and the COVID-19 Pandemic

The COVID-19 pandemic accelerated the adoption of contactless payment methods. Concerns about hygiene and social distancing led to a surge in the use of contactless cards and mobile payments. The convenience and safety of contactless payments have made them a preferred method for many consumers, further entrenching digital payment systems in everyday transactions.

The Future of Digital Payment Systems

The future of digital payment systems looks promising, with continuous advancements in technology and innovation. Emerging technologies like **artificial intelligence (AI)**, **machine learning**, and **biometrics** are expected to enhance the security and convenience of digital payments. AI can provide personalized financial services, detect fraudulent activities, and streamline payment processes.

The integration of **Internet of Things (IoT)** devices into payment systems is another exciting development. IoT-enabled devices can facilitate seamless transactions, such as smart refrigerators that reorder groceries automatically or connected cars that pay for fuel or tolls.

Moreover, the continued growth of cryptocurrencies and central bank digital currencies (CBDCs) will likely shape the future of digital payments. CBDCs are digital forms of fiat currency issued by central banks, offering the benefits of digital payments while maintaining government control and regulation.

CHAPTER 2

The digital payment market has seen tremendous growth and transformation over the past decade. As consumers increasingly prefer cashless transactions for their convenience and security, various platforms have emerged as key players in this space. Among these, Venmo, Cash App, and Apple Pay stand out for their widespread adoption and innovative features. This section explores these major players, their unique offerings, and their impact on the digital payment landscape.

Key Players in the Digital Payment Market: Venmo, Cash App, Apple Pay, and More

Venmo, a subsidiary of PayPal, has become a household name in the peer-to-peer (P2P) payment market. Launched in 2009, Venmo allows users to send money to friends and family using a mobile app. It gained popularity for its social media-like interface, where users can add comments and emojis to transactions, making the payment process more engaging and social.

Venmo's ease of use and integration with bank accounts and credit cards have made it a favorite among millennials and Gen Z. Users can split bills, pay for services, and even purchase goods from select merchants. Venmo also introduced a debit card linked to users' balances, enabling them to use their Venmo funds directly for purchases. As of 2021, Venmo had over 70 million users, illustrating its significant impact on the digital payment market.

Cash App, developed by Square, Inc., is another major player in the P2P payment space. Launched in 2013, Cash App allows users to transfer money to others using a mobile app. It differentiates itself with features like the ability to buy and sell Bitcoin, invest in stocks, and set up direct deposits, making it more than just a payment app.

Cash App has gained traction due to its simplicity and additional financial services. Users can get a Cash Card, a customizable debit card linked to their Cash App balance, which can be used for in-store and online purchases. Cash App's integration with cryptocurrency trading has also attracted a younger, tech-savvy demographic interested in digital assets. By the end of 2020, Cash App had over 30 million active monthly users.

Apple Pay is a mobile payment and digital wallet service by Apple Inc. Launched in 2014, it allows users to make payments in person, in iOS apps, and on the web using Safari. Apple Pay is integrated with Apple devices such as the iPhone, iPad, Apple Watch, and Mac, providing a seamless payment experience across the Apple ecosystem.

Apple Pay uses Near Field Communication (NFC) technology for contactless payments, making transactions quick and secure. The service also supports online purchases and in-app payments, offering a versatile solution for various payment needs. Apple Pay's security features, such as biometric authentication and tokenization, have contributed to its widespread adoption. As of 2021, Apple Pay was accepted by over 85% of U.S. retailers, demonstrating its broad reach and influence.

Google Pay (formerly Google Wallet) is a digital wallet platform and online payment system developed by Google. Launched in 2018, Google Pay consolidates Google's previous payment services under one brand, offering a comprehensive solution for both online and in-store payments.

Google Pay supports contactless payments using NFC technology, similar to Apple Pay. It also allows users to send and receive money, pay bills, and store loyalty cards and tickets. Google Pay's integration with other Google services, such as Gmail and Google Assistant, enhances its functionality and convenience. As of 2020, Google Pay had over 150 million active users across 42 countries, making it one of the most widely used digital payment platforms.

PayPal is one of the oldest and most established players in the digital payment market. Founded in 1998, PayPal provides a platform for online money transfers and serves as an electronic alternative to traditional paper methods like checks and money orders. It allows users to link their bank accounts, credit cards, or PayPal balances to make secure online payments.

PayPal's versatility extends beyond P2P payments to include business transactions, enabling merchants to accept payments from customers worldwide. Its subsidiary services, such as Venmo and Braintree, expand its reach and capabilities. As of 2021, PayPal had over 392 million active accounts, highlighting its dominance in the digital payment market.

Samsung Pay is a mobile payment and digital wallet service by Samsung Electronics. Launched in 2015, Samsung Pay stands out for its use of both NFC and Magnetic Secure Transmission (MST) technology. MST allows Samsung Pay to be used with traditional magnetic stripe terminals, providing broader compatibility compared to other mobile payment services.

Samsung Pay's extensive compatibility and ease of use have contributed to its growing user base. The service also supports online and in-app purchases, as well as P2P transfers. Samsung Pay's integration with Samsung Rewards further incentivizes its use, offering points for transactions that can be redeemed for various rewards. As of 2020, Samsung Pay was available in 29 countries and had millions of active users globally.

In China, **WeChat Pay** and **Alipay** dominate the digital payment market. **WeChat Pay**, integrated into the popular messaging app WeChat, and **Alipay**, owned by Ant Financial, offer comprehensive payment solutions that extend beyond simple transactions.

WeChat Pay allows users to make payments, transfer money, pay bills, and even invest in financial products within the WeChat app. Its integration with social media features makes it a powerful tool for P2P payments and e-commerce.

Alipay offers similar functionalities, including online payments, money transfers, bill payments, and financial services like loans and investments. Alipay's QR code payment system is widely used in China, making it an essential part of everyday transactions. Together, WeChat Pay and Alipay account for over 90% of the mobile payment market in China, illustrating their massive influence and adoption.

Impact on the Digital Payment Landscape

The key players in the digital payment market have significantly impacted how people conduct financial transactions. Their innovations have led to increased convenience, security, and accessibility in payments, driving the shift towards a cashless society.

Convenience and User Experience: The success of digital payment platforms like Venmo, Cash App, and Apple Pay can be attributed to their user-friendly interfaces and seamless integration with other services. These platforms have simplified the process of sending money, making purchases, and managing finances, enhancing the overall user experience.

Security: Security is a major concern for digital payments, and leading platforms have implemented robust measures to protect users' financial information. Features like biometric authentication, encryption, and tokenization help safeguard transactions, building trust among users.

Financial Inclusion: Digital payment platforms have also played a crucial role in promoting financial inclusion. By providing easy access to financial services through mobile devices, these platforms have enabled individuals without traditional bank accounts to participate in the digital economy.

Economic Impact: The widespread adoption of digital payment systems has had a significant economic impact. It has facilitated e-commerce growth, streamlined business transactions, and reduced the costs associated with cash handling and processing. Additionally, digital payments have enabled the rise of new business models and financial services, driving innovation and economic growth.

Global Reach: The global reach of digital payment platforms has connected consumers and businesses across borders, making international transactions easier and more efficient. This has expanded market opportunities for businesses and provided consumers with more choices and convenience.

Chapter 3

The Financial Habits of Gen Alpha and Gen Z

Generations Alpha and Z are reshaping the social, economic, and cultural landscapes with their unique characteristics and preferences. Born into an era of rapid technological advancement, these generations exhibit distinct behaviors, attitudes, and expectations. Understanding their characteristics and preferences is crucial for businesses, educators, policymakers, and marketers aiming to engage with these influential groups.

Who Are Gen Alpha and Gen Z?

Gen Z refers to individuals born between 1997 and 2012. They are the first generation to grow up with the internet and digital technology as integral parts of their daily lives. **Gen Alpha**, born from 2013 onwards, is the youngest generation, currently in their early childhood and adolescence. They are growing up in a world dominated by smartphones, artificial intelligence, and constant connectivity.

Generations Alpha and Z are reshaping the social, economic,

and cultural landscapes with their unique characteristics and preferences. Born into an era of rapid technological advancement, these generations exhibit distinct behaviors, attitudes, and expectations. Understanding their characteristics and preferences is crucial for businesses, educators, policymakers, and marketers aiming to engage with these influential groups.

Characteristics of Gen Z

1. **Digital Natives**: Gen Z is the first true generation of digital natives. They have never known a world without the internet, smartphones, and social media. This digital immersion has shaped their communication styles, learning preferences, and consumer behaviors. They are adept at using multiple digital platforms and are comfortable navigating between them seamlessly.
2. **Tech-Savvy**: Gen Z's tech-savviness extends beyond basic digital literacy. They are proficient in using advanced technologies, including augmented reality (AR), virtual reality (VR), and artificial intelligence (AI). Their familiarity with these technologies influences their expectations for digital experiences, both in their personal lives and in their interactions with brands.
3. **Socially Conscious**: Gen Z is highly aware of social and environmental issues. They prioritize sustainability, diversity, and social justice in their personal and purchasing decisions. According to a 2020 survey by **Deloitte**, 77% of Gen Z respondents said that a company's level of social responsibility affects their purchasing decisions. This generation values authenticity and transparency from brands and expects them to take a stand on important

issues.

4. **Financially Cautious**: Having witnessed the financial struggles of their parents during the Great Recession, Gen Z tends to be more financially cautious. They prioritize saving over spending and are skeptical of debt. A study by the **Center for Generational Kinetics** found that 21% of Gen Z started saving for retirement before the age of 18. This financial prudence extends to their approach to education, with many considering the return on investment for their college degrees.
5. **Entrepreneurial**: Gen Z has a strong entrepreneurial spirit. They are more likely to pursue side hustles, freelance work, and start their own businesses. The gig economy appeals to them because of its flexibility and the ability to balance multiple interests. A report by **Morning Consult** found that nearly half of Gen Z respondents (48%) had already taken on some form of freelance work.

Preferences of Gen Z

1. **Mobile First**: Gen Z prefers mobile-first experiences. They use their smartphones for almost everything, from communication and entertainment to shopping and banking. Businesses targeting Gen Z need to ensure their websites and apps are mobile-friendly and provide seamless experiences across devices.
2. **Visual and Interactive Content**: Gen Z favors visual and interactive content over text-based information. Platforms like Instagram, Snapchat, and TikTok are popular among this generation because they offer rich visual experiences. Brands that leverage video content, AR, and VR are more

likely to capture their attention.
3. **Instant Gratification**: Growing up in an on-demand culture, Gen Z expects instant gratification. They prefer services that offer speed and convenience, such as same-day delivery, streaming services, and real-time customer support. Businesses need to streamline their processes to meet these expectations.
4. **Authenticity and Transparency**: Gen Z values authenticity and transparency from brands. They are quick to identify and reject insincere marketing efforts. Brands that communicate openly, admit mistakes, and take genuine actions on social and environmental issues resonate more with this generation.

Characteristics of Gen Alpha

1. **Digitally Immersed from Birth**: Gen Alpha is the first generation to be fully born in the 21st century, with technology deeply embedded in their lives from birth. They are growing up with voice assistants like Alexa and Google Home, smart devices, and personalized digital content. This immersion in technology is likely to shape their learning and social behaviors significantly.
2. **Highly Educated**: Gen Alpha is projected to be the most formally educated generation in history. They are benefiting from advancements in educational technology, personalized learning, and increased access to information. Digital literacy will be a core component of their education, equipping them with the skills needed for future careers.
3. **Influence of AI and Automation**: Gen Alpha will be the first generation to grow up with widespread AI and automation.

These technologies will influence various aspects of their lives, from personalized learning experiences to automated household chores. Their familiarity with AI will shape their expectations for efficiency and customization in products and services.
4. **Global Awareness**: Growing up in a globally connected world, Gen Alpha will have a broader awareness of global issues and cultures. This global perspective will influence their values, interests, and career choices. They are likely to be more open-minded and inclusive, valuing diversity and cross-cultural experiences.

Preferences of Gen Alpha

1. **Interactive and Gamified Learning**: Gen Alpha prefers interactive and gamified learning experiences. Educational apps and platforms that incorporate game-like elements, such as rewards and challenges, engage them more effectively. This preference for interactive content extends to entertainment and media consumption as well.
2. **Tech-Integrated Toys and Activities**: Gen Alpha enjoys tech-integrated toys and activities. Products like programmable robots, VR gaming systems, and STEM kits appeal to their curiosity and love for technology. These toys not only entertain but also educate, fostering skills in coding, problem-solving, and creativity.
3. **On-Demand Content**: Similar to Gen Z, Gen Alpha expects on-demand content. They are accustomed to streaming services where they can access their favorite shows, music, and games instantly. Brands targeting Gen Alpha need to provide immediate access to high-quality, engaging

content.
4. **Parental Involvement**: While Gen Alpha is highly independent in navigating technology, parental involvement remains significant. Parents often guide their media consumption, educational activities, and online interactions. Brands that cater to both children and their parents, ensuring safety and quality, are likely to succeed.

Early Adoption of Technology and Digital Financial Tools

The rapid advancement of technology has profoundly impacted the financial industry, transforming how individuals and businesses manage, transact, and invest their money. Among the various demographic groups, Gen Z and Gen Alpha stand out as early adopters of digital financial tools. This early adoption is driven by their comfort with technology, the need for convenience, and a desire for more control over their finances. Understanding how these generations are leveraging technology for financial management provides insights into the future of financial services and the broader economy.

Gen Z and Gen Alpha: Digital Natives

Gen Z (born between 1997 and 2012) and Gen Alpha (born from 2013 onwards) are the first generations to grow up with the internet, smartphones, and a plethora of digital tools as an integral part of their daily lives. This early exposure to technology has cultivated a natural proficiency and comfort with digital interfaces, making them adept at navigating various online platforms.

According to a report by **Pew Research Center** (2019), 95% of teens have access to a smartphone, and 45% are online almost constantly. This constant connectivity has influenced their expectations for instant access to information and services, including financial tools. They seek seamless, user-friendly experiences and are quick to adopt technologies that meet these expectations.

Digital Wallets and Mobile Payment Apps

Digital wallets and mobile payment apps are among the most popular financial tools adopted by Gen Z and Gen Alpha. Platforms such as **Apple Pay**, **Google Pay**, **Venmo**, and **Cash App** have revolutionized the way these generations handle transactions. These tools offer convenience, speed, and security, aligning well with the preferences of digital natives.

A study by **Javelin Strategy & Research** (2020) found that 63% of Gen Z individuals use mobile wallets, compared to 51% of millennials. This higher adoption rate is indicative of Gen Z's reliance on mobile technology for financial management. Mobile wallets allow users to store payment information securely, facilitating quick and easy transactions both online and in-store.

Venmo, a subsidiary of PayPal, has become particularly popular among Gen Z for its social features. Users can share payment activities with friends, adding comments and emojis, which makes the financial transactions more engaging. According to **Business Insider Intelligence** (2019), Venmo had over 40 million active users, a significant portion of whom are Gen Z.

Investment Apps and Platforms

The democratization of investing through digital platforms has also appealed to younger generations. Apps like **Robinhood**, **Acorns**, and **Stash** have lowered the barriers to entry for investing, allowing users to start with minimal capital and providing educational resources to guide new investors.

Robinhood, in particular, has been a game-changer. It offers commission-free trading and an easy-to-use interface, making it accessible to novice investors. A **Charles Schwab** survey (2020) found that 70% of Gen Z respondents were interested in investing, and 54% had already opened a brokerage account. Robinhood's success is attributed to its mobile-first approach and features like fractional shares, which allow users to invest in expensive stocks with as little as $1.

Acorns targets a different segment by focusing on micro-investing. It rounds up users' purchases to the nearest dollar and invests the spare change in diversified portfolios. This approach appeals to Gen Z's preference for automated and passive investment strategies. According to **Acorns** (2020), the platform has over 8 million users, with a significant number being young adults and first-time investors.

Budgeting and Personal Finance Apps

Budgeting and personal finance apps have become essential tools for Gen Z and Gen Alpha, helping them manage their money effectively. Apps like **Mint**, **YNAB (You Need a Budget)**, and **PocketGuard** offer features that track spending, set financial goals, and provide insights into financial habits.

Mint, owned by Intuit, aggregates users' financial information from various accounts to provide a comprehensive view of their finances. It offers budgeting tools, bill tracking, and credit score monitoring. A **NerdWallet** survey (2019) revealed that 65% of Gen Z use budgeting apps to manage their finances, highlighting the importance of digital tools in their financial lives.

YNAB takes a proactive approach to budgeting by encouraging users to allocate every dollar to a specific category, promoting mindful spending. The app's emphasis on financial education and goal-setting resonates with Gen Z's desire for financial independence and control.

Cryptocurrency and Blockchain Technology

The rise of cryptocurrency and blockchain technology has also captured the interest of younger generations. Platforms like **Coinbase**, **Binance**, and **BlockFi** have made it easier for individuals to buy, sell, and store cryptocurrencies. Gen Z, in particular, is drawn to the decentralized nature of cryptocurrencies and the potential for high returns.

According to a survey by **Gemini** (2021), 14% of Gen Z respondents reported owning cryptocurrency, and 42% expressed interest in investing in digital assets. This interest is driven by the desire for financial innovation and the appeal of participating in a new and rapidly evolving market.

Coinbase, one of the largest cryptocurrency exchanges, has simplified the process of buying and managing digital assets. Its user-friendly interface and educational resources make it accessible to novice investors. The platform reported having over 56 million verified users in 2021, with a growing number of young investors.

The Role of Social Media

Social media platforms play a significant role in shaping the financial behaviors of Gen Z and Gen Alpha. Financial influencers, or "finfluencers," use platforms like **YouTube**, **Instagram**, and **TikTok** to share tips on budgeting, investing, and using financial tools. This peer-to-peer education model resonates with younger audiences and provides an alternative to traditional financial advice.

A **Pew Research Center** report (2021) found that 45% of teens use YouTube to learn new skills, including financial management. Finfluencers like Graham Stephan, Andrei Jikh, and Tori Dunlap have amassed large followings by offering accessible and relatable financial content. Their influence extends to promoting financial products and services, driving adoption among their followers.

Financial Education and Literacy

The early adoption of digital financial tools by Gen Z and Gen Alpha underscores the importance of financial education. Schools and educational institutions are incorporating financial literacy into their curricula to equip students with the skills needed to navigate the digital financial landscape.

Programs like **Next Gen Personal Finance** provide resources and training for educators to teach personal finance. According to a study by the **Council for Economic Education** (2020), 21 states in the U.S. now require high school students to take a course in economics or personal finance. This focus on financial education is critical for fostering responsible financial behaviors and empowering the next generation of consumers.

The Future of Digital Financial Tools

As technology continues to evolve, the future of digital financial tools looks promising. Innovations such as artificial intelligence (AI), machine learning, and blockchain technology are expected to enhance the functionality and security of financial tools. AI-powered chatbots and robo-advisors are already providing personalized financial advice and management, making it easier for users to achieve their financial goals.

The integration of financial tools with other aspects of daily life, such as smart home devices and wearable technology, will further streamline financial management. For example, voice-activated assistants like **Amazon Alexa** and **Google Assistant** can help users check account balances, pay bills, and set financial reminders.

Comparative Analysis of Gen Alpha and Gen Z with Previous Generations

The emergence of Gen Alpha and Gen Z, born into a world of advanced technology and unprecedented connectivity, marks a significant shift in societal behaviors, values, and expectations. To understand these younger generations better, it is essential to compare them with previous generations: Baby Boomers, Gen X, and Millennials. This comparative analysis examines key differences in technology use, financial behaviors, work preferences, social values, and consumer habits, highlighting how Gen Alpha and Gen Z are shaping the future.

Technology Use

Baby Boomers (born 1946-1964) and **Gen X** (born 1965-1980) grew up in a predominantly analog world, transitioning to digital technology later in life. While Baby Boomers witnessed the advent of television and the early stages of computer technology, Gen X experienced the rise of personal computers and the internet during their formative years. They adapted to digital technology as adults, making them digital immigrants.

In contrast, **Millennials** (born 1981-1996) grew up alongside the internet and witnessed the rapid evolution of mobile technology. They are comfortable with digital devices and social media but still remember a time before smartphones.

Gen Z and **Gen Alpha**, however, are true digital natives. Gen Z was born into a world where the internet was already ubiquitous, and smartphones were common. Gen Alpha, the first generation entirely born in the 21st century, has been surrounded by digital technology from birth, including smart devices, voice assistants, and AI.

A **Pew Research Center** report (2018) highlighted that 95%

of teenagers (Gen Z) have access to a smartphone, and 45% are online almost constantly. This constant connectivity has shaped their communication styles, learning preferences, and consumer behaviors. In comparison, only 68% of Baby Boomers and 85% of Gen X use smartphones, according to a **Pew Research Center** report (2019).

Financial Behaviors

Baby Boomers are known for their conservative financial habits, valuing job stability and long-term investments. They benefited from economic prosperity in their early careers, which influenced their preference for traditional banking and retirement savings.

Gen X faced economic challenges, including the stock market crash of 1987 and the dot-com bubble, leading to a mix of conservative and risk-taking financial behaviors. They value financial independence and are cautious with debt, influenced by witnessing their parents' financial struggles.

Millennials experienced the Great Recession early in their careers, leading to financial instability and a delay in achieving traditional milestones such as homeownership. They are characterized by their use of digital financial tools, student debt burden, and a preference for experiences over material possessions.

Gen Z and **Gen Alpha** have been shaped by the digital economy and financial innovations. Gen Z, in particular, is more financially cautious, prioritizing savings and skeptical of debt. A study by the **Center for Generational Kinetics** (2019) found that 21% of Gen Z started saving for retirement before the age of 18. They use budgeting apps like **Mint** and investment platforms like **Robinhood** to manage their finances.

In contrast, Gen Alpha's financial behaviors are still emerging, but they are expected to be even more adept at using digital financial tools, influenced by their parents' and older siblings' experiences.

Work Preferences

Baby Boomers valued job security and loyalty to employers, often staying with the same company for decades. Their work ethic is characterized by dedication and a preference for hierarchical organizational structures.

Gen X introduced the concept of work-life balance, seeking flexibility and valuing career progression. They are known for their independent and entrepreneurial spirit, often prioritizing results over hours worked.

Millennials disrupted traditional work environments with their preference for flexible hours, remote work, and meaningful work experiences. They value collaboration, purpose, and the integration of technology into the workplace.

Gen Z continues the trend of valuing flexibility but with a stronger emphasis on digital tools and remote work. According to a report by **Dell Technologies** (2019), 80% of Gen Z aspire to work with cutting-edge technology, and 91% say technology would influence their job choice. They value career growth opportunities and diverse work environments.

Gen Alpha is still too young to define their work preferences, but they are expected to demand even greater flexibility, technological integration, and personalized career paths.

Social Values

Baby Boomers experienced significant social changes, including civil rights movements and gender equality advancements. They tend to have more traditional values, influenced by the post-World War II era's economic and social stability.

Gen X grew up during a time of political and economic upheaval, leading to a pragmatic and skeptical outlook. They value individualism and self-reliance, often questioning authority and traditional institutions.

Millennials are known for their progressive social values, advocating for diversity, inclusivity, and environmental sustainability. They have driven the growth of the gig economy and value corporate social responsibility.

Gen Z is even more socially conscious, with a strong emphasis on mental health, gender equality, and climate change. A **Deloitte** (2020) survey found that 77% of Gen Z respondents say a company's level of social responsibility affects their purchasing decisions. They demand authenticity and transparency from brands and are quick to mobilize for social causes.

Gen Alpha will likely inherit these values, growing up in an era where social and environmental issues are at the forefront. They are expected to advocate for sustainability, inclusivity, and global cooperation.

Consumer Habits

Baby Boomers prefer traditional shopping methods, valuing in-store experiences and brand loyalty. They are less influenced by digital marketing and more by brand reputation and personal recommendations.

Gen X balances between traditional and digital shopping. They appreciate the convenience of online shopping but still value the tactile experience of in-store purchases. They are brand loyal but open to new experiences and products.

Millennials have driven the rise of e-commerce, valuing convenience, speed, and personalized experiences. They are influenced by online reviews, social media, and influencer marketing. Their preference for experiences over possessions has fueled the growth of the sharing economy and subscription services.

Gen Z takes digital shopping to the next level, expecting seamless omnichannel experiences. They use social media platforms like Instagram, TikTok, and YouTube for product discovery and purchase. A **Nielsen** (2019) report found that 55% of Gen Z make purchases using their mobile devices, compared to 31% of Gen X.

Gen Alpha will likely continue this trend, with a stronger emphasis on augmented reality (AR) and virtual reality (VR) shopping experiences. They will expect brands to be tech-savvy, engaging, and socially responsible.

4

Chapter 4

Popular Digital Wallets and Payment Apps Among Youth

The digital payments landscape has undergone a radical transformation over the past decade. With the rise of mobile technology and the internet, platforms like **Venmo**, **Cash App**, **Apple Pay**, and others have revolutionized how we conduct financial transactions. These platforms offer varying features and cater to different user needs, yet all share the common goal of simplifying and securing the way we manage and transfer money. This in-depth analysis explores the functionalities, user base, market impact, and future prospects of these leading digital payment platforms.

Venmo

Venmo, a subsidiary of PayPal, has become a household name in peer-to-peer (P2P) payments. Launched in 2009, Venmo allows users to send money to friends and family using a mobile app. Its social media-like interface, where users can add comments and emojis to transactions, differentiates it from other payment platforms by making the payment process more engaging and social.

Functionality and Features

Venmo offers a range of features that cater to its young, tech-savvy user base:

- **P2P Payments**: Users can easily send and receive money from friends and family.
- **Venmo Debit Card**: Linked to the user's Venmo balance, this card can be used for purchases anywhere Mastercard is accepted.
- **Direct Deposit**: Users can have their paychecks directly deposited into their Venmo account.
- **Pay with Venmo**: This feature allows users to make purchases at select online retailers using their Venmo balance.

Venmo also integrates with various apps and services, such as Uber and Grubhub, allowing users to make payments directly through these platforms.

User Base and Market Impact

As of 2021, Venmo had over 70 million active users, with a significant portion being millennials and Gen Z. Its popularity among younger users is attributed to its ease of use, social features, and integration with everyday services. Venmo processed approximately $230 billion in total payment volume in 2020, demonstrating its significant impact on the digital payments market.

Future Prospects

Venmo continues to innovate by expanding its offerings. It recently introduced a feature that allows users to buy, hold, and sell cryptocurrencies directly within the app. This move aligns with the growing interest in digital currencies among younger generations and positions Venmo as a more comprehensive financial tool.

Cash App

Cash App, developed by Square, Inc., is another major player in the P2P payment space. Launched in 2013, Cash App allows users to transfer money to others using a mobile app. It differentiates itself with features like the ability to buy and sell Bitcoin, invest in stocks, and set up direct deposits.

Functionality and Features

Cash App offers a robust set of features:

- **P2P Payments**: Users can send and receive money quickly and easily.
- **Cash Card**: A customizable debit card linked to the user's Cash App balance, usable for in-store and online purchases.
- **Bitcoin Trading**: Users can buy and sell Bitcoin directly within the app.
- **Stock Investing**: Cash App allows users to invest in stocks with no commission fees.
- **Direct Deposit**: Users can receive their paychecks directly into their Cash App account.

Cash App also provides banking features, such as setting up a routing and account number to facilitate direct deposits and bill payments.

User Base and Market Impact

By the end of 2020, Cash App had over 36 million active users. Its simplicity and additional financial services have made it a popular choice among younger demographics. Cash App processed $41 billion in gross profit in 2020, illustrating its strong market presence.

Future Prospects

Cash App is continuously expanding its functionalities. The integration of banking services, investment options, and cryptocurrency trading makes it a versatile financial tool. Future developments may include more comprehensive banking services and enhanced investment features.

Apple Pay

Apple Pay is a mobile payment and digital wallet service by Apple Inc., launched in 2014. It allows users to make payments in person, in iOS apps, and on the web using Safari. Apple Pay is integrated with Apple devices such as the iPhone, iPad, Apple Watch, and Mac, providing a seamless payment experience across the Apple ecosystem.

Functionality and Features

Apple Pay leverages Near Field Communication (NFC) technology for contactless payments, making transactions quick and secure:

- **Contactless Payments**: Users can make payments by tapping their device at contactless terminals.
- **In-App and Online Purchases**: Apple Pay can be used for purchases within apps and on websites.
- **Apple Card**: A credit card issued by Apple in partnership with Goldman Sachs, integrated with Apple Pay for seamless transactions.
- **Apple Cash**: Users can send and receive money through iMessage, similar to Venmo and Cash App.

Security features include biometric authentication (Face ID, Touch ID), tokenization, and a dedicated Secure Element chip that stores payment information securely.

User Base and Market Impact

As of 2021, Apple Pay was accepted by over 85% of U.S. retailers. It is particularly popular among Apple device users, benefiting from the loyalty and trust associated with the Apple brand. Apple Pay's seamless integration across Apple products has made it a leading mobile payment solution.

Future Prospects

Apple Pay continues to expand its services, including the introduction of Apple Card and Apple Cash. Future prospects may involve deeper integration with other financial services and expanded global reach, leveraging Apple's extensive ecosystem and user base.

Google Pay

Google Pay (formerly Google Wallet) is a digital wallet platform and online payment system developed by Google. Launched in 2018, Google Pay consolidates Google's previous payment services under one brand, offering a comprehensive solution for both online and in-store payments.

Functionality and Features

Google Pay supports contactless payments using NFC technology, similar to Apple Pay:

- **Contactless Payments**: Users can make payments by tapping their device at contactless terminals.
- **In-App and Online Purchases**: Google Pay can be used for purchases within apps and on websites.
- **Peer-to-Peer Payments**: Users can send and receive money through the app.
- **Integration with Google Services**: Google Pay integrates with Gmail and Google Assistant, enhancing its functional-

ity.

Google Pay also offers features like storing loyalty cards, boarding passes, and tickets, providing a convenient all-in-one digital wallet.

User Base and Market Impact

As of 2020, Google Pay had over 150 million active users across 42 countries, making it one of the most widely used digital payment platforms. Its integration with the broader Google ecosystem enhances its appeal and functionality.

Future Prospects

Google Pay is continually expanding its services and geographic reach. Future developments may include enhanced security features, more integrations with other Google services, and expanded financial services offerings.

PayPal

PayPal is one of the oldest and most established players in the digital payment market. Founded in 1998, PayPal provides a platform for online money transfers and serves as an electronic alternative to traditional paper methods like checks and money orders.

Functionality and Features

PayPal offers a wide range of services catering to both consumers and businesses:

- **Online Payments**: Users can make purchases online at millions of websites.
- **Peer-to-Peer Payments**: Users can send and receive money from friends and family.
- **Business Services**: PayPal offers invoicing, payment processing, and merchant services for businesses.

- **PayPal Credit**: A line of credit that users can use for purchases and pay off over time.

PayPal's subsidiary services, such as Venmo and Braintree, expand its reach and capabilities, catering to different segments of the market.

User Base and Market Impact

As of 2021, PayPal had over 392 million active accounts, highlighting its dominance in the digital payment market. It processed $936 billion in total payment volume in 2020, demonstrating its significant impact on global commerce.

Future Prospects

PayPal continues to innovate and expand its services. Recent acquisitions, such as Honey, a popular browser extension for finding online deals, and the introduction of cryptocurrency trading, indicate PayPal's commitment to staying at the forefront of digital payments.

Samsung Pay

Samsung Pay is a mobile payment and digital wallet service by Samsung Electronics. Launched in 2015, Samsung Pay stands out for its use of both NFC and Magnetic Secure Transmission (MST) technology. MST allows Samsung Pay to be used with traditional magnetic stripe terminals, providing broader compatibility compared to other mobile payment services.

Functionality and Features

Samsung Pay offers extensive compatibility and a range of features:

- **Contactless Payments**: Users can make payments by tapping their device at contactless terminals.
- **MST Technology**: Enables payments at traditional mag-

netic stripe terminals.
- **In-App and Online Purchases**: Samsung Pay can be used for purchases within apps and on websites.
- **Samsung Rewards**: A loyalty program that offers points for transactions, which can be redeemed for various rewards.

User Base and Market Impact

As of 2020, Samsung Pay was available in 29 countries and had millions of active users globally. Its extensive compatibility and ease of use have contributed to its growing user base and market presence.

Future Prospects

Samsung Pay continues to enhance its services and expand its geographic reach. Future developments may include deeper integration with Samsung's ecosystem of devices and services, offering a more comprehensive digital experience.

Features That Attract Younger Users to Digital Payment Platforms

The rise of digital payment platforms has significantly changed the financial landscape, particularly for younger generations like Gen Z and Gen Alpha. These cohorts have grown up in a world where technology is ubiquitous, shaping their expectations and behaviors. Platforms like **Venmo**, **Cash App**, **Apple Pay**, and others have successfully tapped into this demographic by offering features tailored to their preferences. This comprehensive analysis explores the features that attract younger users to digital payment platforms, delving into the elements that make these services appealing and effective.

Ease of Use and Intuitive Interfaces

One of the primary reasons younger users gravitate towards digital payment platforms is their ease of use and intuitive interfaces. Unlike traditional banking methods, these platforms offer streamlined processes that can be navigated effortlessly through mobile apps.

Venmo, for instance, allows users to send and receive money with just a few taps. The app's clean and simple design, combined with the ability to link bank accounts and credit cards seamlessly, makes financial transactions straightforward and hassle-free. Similarly, **Cash App** offers a user-friendly interface that simplifies the process of transferring money, buying Bitcoin, and investing in stocks. The app's minimalistic design ensures that users can perform these functions without encountering complexity or confusion.

Apple Pay integrates smoothly with Apple devices, utilizing intuitive gestures and the familiar Apple ecosystem to facilitate payments. This seamless integration ensures that users can quickly adapt to using Apple Pay without the need for extensive tutorials or instructions.

Social Integration and Sharing

Social integration is another critical feature that attracts younger users to digital payment platforms. The ability to share transaction details and interact socially within the app adds a layer of engagement that resonates with digitally native generations.

Venmo is particularly known for its social feed, where users can see their friends' transactions (without revealing the amounts) and add comments or emojis. This feature turns a mundane financial transaction into a social interaction, making it more relatable and enjoyable. The social aspect of Venmo mimics the behavior of social media platforms, which are integral to the daily lives of younger users.

Cash App has also embraced social elements, albeit to a lesser extent. The app allows users to create a unique $Cashtag, which can be shared with others for easy payments. This personalization fosters a sense of identity and community within the app.

Instant Gratification and Speed

The desire for instant gratification is a well-documented trait among younger generations, and digital payment platforms cater to this by offering fast, real-time transactions. Waiting for funds to clear is a thing of the past, as these platforms provide immediate access to transferred money.

Venmo and **Cash App** both support instant transfers, allowing users to move money from their app balance to their bank account within minutes for a small fee. This immediacy is crucial for users who need quick access to their funds, whether for splitting bills, making purchases, or emergency situations.

Apple Pay facilitates instant payments at point-of-sale terminals using contactless technology, ensuring that transactions are completed swiftly and efficiently. The use of Near Field Communication (NFC) technology allows users to make payments with just a tap of their device, catering to the need for speed and convenience.

Enhanced Security Features

Security is a top priority for digital payment platforms, especially when targeting younger users who are often more cautious about online safety. These platforms incorporate advanced security features to protect user data and transactions, fostering trust and confidence.

Venmo uses encryption and multi-factor authentication to secure transactions. Additionally, users can set up a PIN code or biometric authentication (fingerprint or facial recognition) to access the app, adding an extra layer of security.

Cash App employs similar security measures, including encryption and PIN protection. The app also allows users to disable their Cash Card if it is lost or stolen, providing peace of mind.

Apple Pay stands out with its robust security infrastructure. The platform uses tokenization to replace card details with a unique identifier, ensuring that actual card information is never shared with merchants. Biometric authentication via Face ID or Touch ID further secures transactions, making Apple Pay one of the safest digital payment options available.

Personalization and Customization

Personalization and customization are highly valued by younger users, and digital payment platforms have capitalized on this by offering various ways to tailor the user experience.

Cash App allows users to customize their Cash Card with different colors, designs, and even a signature or drawing. This feature enhances user engagement by letting them express their individuality through their payment methods.

Venmo offers limited customization options, such as the ability to add a profile picture and create personalized usernames. These features, while not extensive, still provide a sense of identity and personalization.

Apple Pay integrates with the broader Apple ecosystem, allowing users to personalize their payment experience through their Apple ID and associated preferences. The ability to choose default payment methods and manage multiple cards within the Wallet app provides a tailored experience that aligns with individual user needs.

Integration with Other Financial Services

Integration with other financial services is a feature that significantly enhances the appeal of digital payment platforms. Younger users appreciate having access to a suite of financial tools within a single app, streamlining their financial management.

Cash App excels in this area by offering stock trading and Bitcoin transactions in addition to its core P2P payment functionality. Users can buy and sell stocks without paying commissions and trade Bitcoin directly within the app. This integration of services makes Cash App a comprehensive financial tool for young investors.

Venmo has also expanded its services to include Venmo Credit Card and Venmo Business profiles, catering to both individual users and small businesses. These additions provide users with more options to manage their finances within the Venmo ecosystem.

Apple Pay integrates with Apple Card, a credit card issued by Apple in partnership with Goldman Sachs. The Apple Card offers daily cashback rewards and is managed through the Wallet app, providing a seamless and integrated financial experience. Additionally, Apple Pay supports transit cards and other payment options, making it a versatile tool for various financial needs.

Gamification and Rewards

Gamification and rewards are effective strategies to engage younger users, and digital payment platforms have incorporated these elements to boost user activity and loyalty.

Venmo periodically offers promotions and cashback deals for using the Venmo Debit Card at select merchants. These incentives encourage users to utilize Venmo more frequently and explore its various features.

Cash App uses gamification through its "Cash Boost" feature, which offers instant discounts at certain retailers when users pay with their Cash Card. This feature not only provides savings but also incentivizes users to choose Cash App for their purchases.

Apple Pay integrates with the Apple Card's rewards system, offering daily cashback on purchases. This immediate reward system appeals to the younger generation's preference for instant gratification and adds value to using Apple Pay for everyday transactions.

Customer Support and Community Engagement

Responsive customer support and community engagement are essential for retaining younger users, who expect prompt assistance and value community interactions.

Venmo offers customer support through various channels, including in-app chat, email, and social media. The company also maintains a robust presence on social media platforms, engaging with users and addressing their concerns in real-time.

Cash App provides customer support via in-app messaging and email. The app's extensive help section includes sections and FAQs to assist users in troubleshooting common issues. Cash App also actively engages with its community through social media, fostering a sense of belonging and support.

Apple Pay benefits from Apple's extensive customer support infrastructure, including 24/7 support via phone, chat, and email. Apple's commitment to customer service ensures that users can quickly resolve any issues they encounter, enhancing their overall experience.

Case Studies of Usage Patterns and Preferences in Digital Payment Platforms

Digital payment platforms have become integral to the financial habits of users across various demographics. By examining the usage patterns and preferences of different groups, we can gain valuable insights into how these platforms are utilized and what features resonate most with users. This section delves into several case studies, focusing on **Venmo**, **Cash App**, and **Apple Pay**, to understand how these platforms are shaping financial behaviors.

Case Study 1: Venmo and Millennials

Venmo, with its social media-like interface, has become exceptionally popular among millennials. This demographic, typically defined as those born between 1981 and 1996, values convenience, social connectivity, and transparency in their financial transactions.

Usage Patterns

A study by **Business Insider Intelligence** (2019) found that 60% of millennials use Venmo for P2P payments. The platform's integration with social media features—such as the ability to add comments and emojis to transactions—creates a unique social experience. This feature turns mundane financial transactions into social interactions, which appeals to millennials' desire for connectivity and engagement.

Millennials frequently use Venmo for splitting bills, paying rent, and sharing expenses for group activities. The app's simplicity and speed make it ideal for quick, everyday transactions. Additionally, the Venmo Debit Card extends the app's utility by allowing users to spend their Venmo balance directly at merchants.

Preferences

Millennials prefer Venmo for its user-friendly interface and the social feed feature. They appreciate the transparency of seeing transaction histories and the ability to publicly or privately share payments. This demographic also values the security features, such as multi-factor authentication and encryption, which ensure their transactions are safe.

Case Study 2: Cash App and Gen Z

Cash App, developed by Square, Inc., has gained significant traction among Gen Z users, those born between 1997 and 2012. This generation is characterized by their digital nativeness and preference for technology-driven solutions.

Usage Patterns

A report by **Javelin Strategy & Research** (2020) highlighted that 63% of Gen Z individuals use mobile wallets, with Cash App being a top choice. Gen Z users appreciate Cash App's multifunctionality, which includes P2P payments, Bitcoin trading, and stock investing. These additional features make Cash App more than just a payment app; it serves as a comprehensive financial tool.

Gen Z users frequently use Cash App for transferring money among peers, paying for goods and services, and engaging in financial markets. The app's ability to handle Bitcoin transactions appeals to the tech-savvy nature of this generation, who are often early adopters of new financial technologies.

Preferences

Gen Z values Cash App's intuitive interface and the variety of financial services it offers. The ability to buy and sell Bitcoin directly within the app is particularly appealing. The customizable Cash Card, which allows users to personalize their debit card with unique designs and colors, also resonates with this demographic's desire for individuality and personalization.

Case Study 3: Apple Pay and Tech-Savvy Consumers

Apple Pay is favored by tech-savvy consumers who are deeply embedded in the Apple ecosystem. This group includes a wide age range but is unified by their preference for high-tech, integrated solutions.

Usage Patterns

According to a **Statista** report (2021), Apple Pay is used by approximately 383 million people worldwide. Tech-savvy consumers utilize Apple Pay for its convenience and security. The platform allows for contactless payments, which have become increasingly important in the wake of the COVID-19 pandemic.

These users appreciate the seamless integration of Apple Pay with other Apple products. They often use the service for in-store purchases, online shopping, and in-app transactions. The convenience of using devices they already own—like iPhones, Apple Watches, and Macs—enhances their overall user experience.

Preferences

Tech-savvy consumers prefer Apple Pay for its robust security features, such as biometric authentication (Face ID and Touch ID) and tokenization, which replace sensitive card details with unique identifiers. The convenience of making payments with a simple tap or click, without the need to carry physical cards, is also highly valued. Additionally, Apple Pay's integration with Apple Card and Apple Cash provides a comprehensive financial ecosystem that caters to various needs.

Case Study 4: Google Pay in Emerging Markets

Google Pay has seen substantial growth in emerging markets, particularly in India, where digital payments are becoming increasingly prevalent.

Usage Patterns

A **TechCrunch** report (2020) highlighted that Google Pay is one of the leading digital payment platforms in India, with over 67 million monthly active users. The platform's ease of use and wide acceptance have made it popular for a range of transactions, from small everyday purchases to larger business payments.

In emerging markets, users often rely on Google Pay for utility bill payments, mobile recharges, and P2P transfers. The app's ability to link directly with bank accounts via the Unified Payments Interface (UPI) has facilitated widespread adoption, as it simplifies the process of sending and receiving money.

Preferences

Users in emerging markets prefer Google Pay for its reliability, security, and wide acceptance among merchants. The platform's integration with UPI ensures that transactions are fast and free of charge. Additionally, Google Pay's rewards and cashback offers for transactions provide added incentives for users.

Case Study 5: PayPal's Global Reach

PayPal remains a dominant player in the global digital payment landscape, appealing to a diverse user base that spans multiple generations and regions.

Usage Patterns

PayPal is widely used for online shopping, business transactions, and P2P payments. A **Statista** report (2021) noted that PayPal had 392 million active accounts worldwide. The platform's versatility makes it suitable for various financial activities, from paying for goods and services on e-commerce sites to sending money to friends and family.

In addition to individual users, many small and medium-sized businesses rely on PayPal for invoicing and payment processing. The platform's integration with e-commerce platforms like eBay and Shopify has further cemented its position as a trusted payment solution.

Preferences

Users appreciate PayPal for its global acceptance, ease of use, and robust security measures. The platform's buyer and seller protection policies provide additional peace of mind, making it a preferred choice for online transactions. PayPal's ability to handle multiple currencies and international payments seamlessly also appeals to users engaged in cross-border commerce.

Chapter 5

The Influence of Social Media and Peer Networks

The Role of Social Media in Promoting Digital Wallets

In the era of rapid digitalization, social media has emerged as a powerful tool for promoting a variety of products and services, including digital wallets. Platforms such as **Facebook**, **Instagram**, **Twitter**, and **TikTok** are not just venues for social interaction but also dynamic spaces where businesses can reach millions of potential customers. This section explores how social media is instrumental in promoting digital wallets like **Venmo**, **Cash App**, **Apple Pay**, and others, and how these platforms leverage social media to enhance their visibility, user engagement, and adoption rates.

Leveraging Influencers and Social Proof

One of the most effective strategies for promoting digital wallets on social media is leveraging influencers. Influencers, individuals with large followings on social media platforms, can significantly impact the purchasing decisions of their audience. By collaborating with influencers, digital wallet companies can reach a broader audience and build trust more quickly than through traditional advertising methods.

For instance, **Venmo** has successfully used influencer marketing to promote its services. Influencers often share their positive experiences with Venmo, demonstrating how easy and convenient it is to use the app for splitting bills, paying friends, and making purchases. This type of social proof can be incredibly persuasive, as followers are more likely to trust recommendations from people they admire or see as relatable.

According to a survey by **Mediakix** (2019), 89% of marketers find that the return on investment (ROI) from influencer marketing on par or better than other marketing channels. This underscores the effectiveness of influencers in driving engagement and adoption for digital wallets.

Social Media Advertising

Paid advertising on social media platforms is another crucial method for promoting digital wallets. Platforms like Facebook and Instagram offer highly targeted advertising options that allow companies to reach specific demographics based on age, interests, behavior, and location. This precision targeting ensures that promotional content for digital wallets reaches the most relevant audience segments.

Cash App, for example, utilizes Facebook Ads to target users who are likely to be interested in financial services and digital payments. These ads often highlight the app's features, such as instant money transfers, Bitcoin trading, and investing in stocks, catering to the financial interests of the audience. By using eye-catching visuals and compelling copy, Cash App can attract new users and retain existing ones.

The success of social media advertising is supported by data from **Hootsuite** (2020), which shows that 90% of Instagram users follow at least one business, indicating a strong potential for businesses to connect with consumers through this platform.

Viral Marketing and User-Generated Content

Viral marketing and user-generated content (UGC) are powerful tools for promoting digital wallets on social media. UGC, which includes posts, reviews, and testimonials created by users, can enhance the credibility and appeal of digital wallet services. When users share their positive experiences, it creates a ripple effect that can attract more users to the platform.

Venmo's social feed is a prime example of leveraging UGC. The app allows users to share their transactions publicly (without revealing the amount), adding a social dimension to financial transactions. This public feed can make financial interactions feel more communal and fun, encouraging more users to join and engage with the platform.

Similarly, **TikTok** has become a hub for viral marketing campaigns. **Cash App** has capitalized on this by running hashtag challenges and other viral marketing strategies that encourage users to create content featuring the app. These challenges often include incentives, such as cash prizes, which motivate users to participate and spread the word.

A study by **Nielsen** (2020) found that consumers are 92% more likely to trust personal recommendations over traditional advertising, highlighting the importance of UGC and viral marketing in promoting digital wallets.

Engaging Content and Educational Campaigns

Educational content and engaging campaigns are essential for promoting digital wallets, especially as they often involve new or unfamiliar technology. Social media platforms provide an ideal space for digital wallet companies to educate potential users about their services through engaging content.

Apple Pay frequently uses its social media channels to post tutorials and informational videos about how to set up and use its services. These posts often include step-by-step guides, FAQs, and benefits of using Apple Pay, making it easier for users to understand and adopt the technology.

Moreover, **Google Pay** leverages YouTube for detailed video tutorials and customer testimonials, which can demystify the app's features and benefits. By breaking down the process and highlighting the security features, Google Pay helps build user confidence in its service.

Educational campaigns are particularly important for reaching older demographics who may be less familiar with digital wallets. By providing clear and accessible information, digital wallet companies can expand their user base beyond tech-savvy younger generations.

Customer Engagement and Support

Social media platforms are also critical for customer engagement and support. Users often turn to social media to ask questions, resolve issues, and provide feedback. Prompt and helpful responses from digital wallet companies can enhance customer satisfaction and loyalty.

PayPal, for instance, maintains active customer support channels on Twitter and Facebook. Users can tweet at PayPal's support account or send a message through Facebook for assistance. This immediate support helps resolve issues quickly and publicly demonstrates the company's commitment to customer service.

Additionally, by engaging with users on social media, digital wallet companies can gather valuable feedback and insights.

This information can be used to improve services, address common concerns, and develop new features that better meet user needs.

According to **Sprout Social** (2020), 79% of consumers expect a response from brands within 24 hours of reaching out on social media, emphasizing the importance of timely and effective customer engagement.

Building Communities and Fostering Loyalty

Building communities and fostering loyalty are long-term strategies that digital wallet companies use to retain users and encourage repeated use. Social media platforms offer various tools for community building, such as groups, forums, and events.

Venmo and **Cash App** have active communities on platforms like Reddit and Facebook, where users can share tips, ask questions, and discuss their experiences. These communities create a sense of belonging and provide a space for users to connect with others who share similar interests and financial habits.

Loyalty programs are also promoted through social media. For example, **Samsung Pay**'s rewards program is frequently highlighted on its social media channels. Users earn points for transactions, which can be redeemed for various rewards. By promoting these programs on social media, Samsung Pay can keep users engaged and incentivize regular use.

Peer Influence and Viral Trends in Financial Technology Adoption

The adoption of financial technology (fintech) has been significantly shaped by peer influence and viral trends. These factors play a crucial role in how new financial tools and platforms gain traction, especially among younger, tech-savvy generations. This comprehensive analysis explores the impact of peer influence and viral trends on fintech adoption, highlighting the mechanisms through which they operate and the resulting effects on user behavior and market dynamics.

The Power of Peer Influence in Fintech Adoption

Peer influence, or the impact that the behaviors, attitudes, and preferences of friends and acquaintances have on an individual, is a powerful driver of fintech adoption. This phenomenon is particularly strong among millennials and Gen Z, who often look to their social circles for recommendations and endorsements.

Social Proof and Trust

Social proof is a psychological concept where people mimic the actions of others in an attempt to reflect correct behavior in a given situation. In the context of fintech, social proof can be seen when individuals adopt a new financial tool because their peers are using it successfully.

Platforms like **Venmo** and **Cash App** benefit greatly from social proof. When users see their friends and family using these apps to split bills, send money, and make purchases, they are more likely to trust and adopt these tools themselves. This trust is bolstered by the visibility of transactions within social networks, where users can see who is using the app and how it is being used.

According to a study by **Nielsen** (2020), 92% of consumers trust recommendations from friends and family over other forms of advertising. This trust is crucial for fintech companies looking to build a user base, as financial tools inherently require a high level of trust due to the sensitive nature of the information involved.

Network Effects

Network effects occur when a product or service gains additional value as more people use it. This is a significant factor in the adoption of fintech platforms. The more people use a platform like **Venmo**, the more valuable it becomes to its users because they can transact with a larger network of friends and acquaintances.

PayPal and **Zelle** also benefit from network effects. PayPal's widespread acceptance among online merchants and Zelle's integration with major banks in the U.S. make these platforms more attractive as they become more ubiquitous. Users are more likely to adopt these tools if they know that their peers and preferred merchants already accept and use them.

Viral Trends and Their Impact on Fintech Adoption

Viral trends, characterized by rapid and widespread dissemination of information through social media and other online channels, have a profound impact on fintech adoption. These trends can create a sense of urgency and excitement around new financial tools, driving rapid user growth.

Social Media Campaigns

Social media platforms like **Instagram**, **Twitter**, and **TikTok** are fertile ground for viral marketing campaigns. Fintech companies leverage these platforms to reach large audiences quickly and cost-effectively.

For instance, **Cash App** has effectively used Twitter to run viral marketing campaigns, such as #CashAppFriday, where users can win money by following and retweeting the company's posts. This not only drives engagement but also attracts new users who want to participate in these promotions.

Robinhood, a commission-free trading app, has also capitalized on viral trends. During the GameStop trading frenzy in early 2021, Robinhood was at the center of a viral trend that brought millions of new users to the platform. Social media discussions and viral posts played a critical role in driving this surge in adoption.

Influencer Partnerships

Partnering with influencers is another effective strategy for fintech companies. Influencers, with their large and engaged followings, can drive significant traffic and new users to fintech platforms.

Venmo and **Square's Cash App** have both partnered with influencers to promote their services. Influencers create content showcasing how they use these apps in their daily lives, providing relatable and authentic endorsements that resonate with their followers. This strategy leverages the trust and rapport that influencers have built with their audiences.

Viral Challenges and Hashtags

Creating viral challenges and hashtags is a popular method for fintech companies to boost visibility and engagement. By encouraging users to create and share content around a specific theme or challenge, companies can harness the power of user-generated content to drive adoption.

For example, **Cash App** has launched several viral challenges on TikTok, where users can participate by creating videos that highlight the app's features. These challenges often include incentives, such as cash prizes, which further motivate participation and sharing.

CHAPTER 5

The Role of Community and User Engagement

Building a strong community and fostering user engagement are critical components of successful fintech adoption. Platforms that prioritize community-building and user interaction tend to see higher levels of user retention and satisfaction.

Community Forums and Support

Many fintech companies host community forums and support groups where users can share tips, ask questions, and provide feedback. These forums not only help users get the most out of the platform but also create a sense of belonging and community.

Revolut, a digital banking app, has an active community forum where users discuss features, provide feedback, and help each other with issues. This community engagement fosters loyalty and encourages users to stay with the platform.

Gamification and Rewards

Gamification, the application of game-design elements in non-game contexts, is another effective strategy to engage users. Fintech platforms use gamification to make financial management more enjoyable and rewarding.

Acorns, an investment app, uses gamification by showing users their potential future savings growth through engaging visuals and progress trackers. This helps users stay motivated and committed to their investment goals.

Stash, another investment app, offers rewards and educational challenges that help users learn about investing while earning bonuses. This approach not only educates users but also keeps them engaged and active on the platform.

Case Studies: Successful Fintech Adoption through Peer Influence and Viral Trends

Case Study 1: Venmo

Venmo's success can be largely attributed to its social features and peer influence. The app's social feed allows users to see their friends' transactions (without revealing amounts), creating a social experience around financial transactions. This visibility encourages new users to join and engage with the platform.

Venmo also runs targeted social media campaigns and partnerships with influencers to drive adoption. By integrating social proof and leveraging network effects, Venmo has built a robust user base primarily composed of younger, tech-savvy individuals.

Case Study 2: Cash App

Cash App has effectively utilized viral trends and influencer partnerships to boost its user base. Campaigns like #CashAppFriday have gone viral, attracting new users through the promise of cash prizes. Cash App also partners with influencers who showcase the app's features to their followers, driving authentic and relatable endorsements.

Cash App's strategy of integrating various financial services, such as Bitcoin trading and stock investing, has also appealed to a broader audience, making it a versatile financial tool for different needs.

Case Study 3: Robinhood

Robinhood's rise to popularity is a prime example of viral trends influencing fintech adoption. The GameStop trading frenzy, fueled by discussions on Reddit and other social media platforms, brought millions of new users to Robinhood. The app's user-friendly interface and commission-free trading model resonated with young, novice investors looking to capitalize on viral trading trends.

Robinhood's success highlights the power of viral trends in driving rapid adoption and the importance of being responsive to social media dynamics.

Examples of Social Media Campaigns and Their Impact on Digital Wallet Adoption

Social media has become a critical platform for promoting digital wallets, leveraging vast user bases and dynamic engagement tools. This section explores various social media campaigns by digital wallet companies like **Venmo**, **Cash App**, and **Apple Pay**, and examines their impact on user adoption and engagement.

Venmo: Leveraging Social Features and Viral Campaigns

Venmo, known for its social media-like interface, has effectively utilized social features and viral campaigns to boost its user base. One notable example is the integration of Venmo's transaction feed with users' social media networks.

Social Feed Integration

Venmo's transaction feed allows users to share their payment activities with friends, complete with comments and emojis. This feature turns financial transactions into social interactions, akin to posting on Facebook or Instagram. Users can see who their friends are paying and what for, which fosters a sense of community and transparency.

Impact: The social feed has significantly contributed to Venmo's popularity among younger demographics. According to **Business Insider Intelligence** (2019), 60% of millennials use Venmo, demonstrating how the integration of social features can drive user adoption and engagement.

#VenmoItForward Campaign

Venmo launched the #VenmoItForward campaign, encouraging users to perform random acts of kindness using the platform. Participants were asked to share their acts on social media with the hashtag #VenmoItForward, creating a viral trend that showcased the app's ease of use and social benefits.

Impact: The campaign generated significant buzz on platforms like Twitter and Instagram, increasing Venmo's visibility and reinforcing its image as a fun, socially integrated payment solution. The user-generated content from the campaign served as authentic endorsements, attracting new users through social proof.

Cash App: Viral Challenges and Influencer Partnerships

Cash App, developed by Square, Inc., has utilized viral challenges and influencer partnerships to drive user engagement and adoption.

#CashAppFriday

Cash App's #CashAppFriday campaign has become a staple on Twitter, where the company gives away cash to participants who follow and retweet their posts. This simple yet effective campaign leverages the allure of free money to drive massive engagement every week.

Impact: The #CashAppFriday campaign has significantly boosted Cash App's visibility and user engagement. According to **Hootsuite** (2020), the campaign trends weekly on Twitter, reaching millions of users and resulting in a substantial increase in downloads and active users.

Influencer Partnerships

Cash App has partnered with numerous influencers and celebrities to promote its services. For example, popular hip-hop artists like Travis Scott and Megan Thee Stallion have collaborated with Cash App to run giveaway campaigns and promote the app to their followers.

Impact: These partnerships have helped Cash App tap into the influencers' fan bases, attracting a younger, tech-savvy audience. Influencers' authentic endorsements and the virality of their posts have led to increased downloads and usage of Cash App, particularly among Gen Z and millennials.

Apple Pay: Educational Campaigns and Strategic Integrations

Apple Pay has focused on educational campaigns and strategic integrations to promote its digital wallet service.

Apple Pay Tutorials on Social Media

Apple Pay has used its social media channels to post tutorials and informational videos about setting up and using Apple Pay. These posts often include step-by-step guides, FAQs, and highlight the security features of the platform.

Impact: These educational campaigns have demystified the process of using Apple Pay, making it more accessible to a broader audience. By addressing potential users' concerns and demonstrating the platform's ease of use, Apple Pay has increased its adoption rates, particularly among users who may be less familiar with digital wallets.

Integration with Apple Ecosystem

Apple Pay's integration with the broader Apple ecosystem, including promotions on Apple's official social media accounts, has also played a crucial role in its adoption. Announcements and updates about Apple Pay's new features or partnerships are shared across Apple's social media channels, reaching millions of users instantly.

Impact: The strategic use of Apple's social media presence has helped maintain a consistent and cohesive brand message, reinforcing Apple Pay's security, convenience, and seamless integration with other Apple products. This has contributed to the platform's growth and acceptance among Apple's loyal customer base.

Google Pay: Regional Campaigns and UPI Integration in India

Google Pay has effectively used regional campaigns and its integration with the Unified Payments Interface (UPI) in India to drive adoption.

#GooglePayIt Campaign

In India, Google Pay launched the #GooglePayIt campaign to encourage users to adopt digital payments. The campaign featured popular Bollywood actors and cricket stars, who demonstrated the convenience and benefits of using Google Pay for everyday transactions.

Impact: The #GooglePayIt campaign resonated well with the Indian audience, leveraging the influence of local celebrities to build trust and familiarity. This, combined with the ease of UPI integration, led to a surge in Google Pay users, making it one of the leading digital payment platforms in India. According to **TechCrunch** (2020), Google Pay had over 67 million monthly active users in India following the campaign.

Festive Season Promotions

During major Indian festivals, Google Pay runs special promotions and cashback offers, encouraging users to make payments using the app. These promotions are heavily advertised on social media platforms like Facebook, Instagram, and YouTube.

Impact: Festive season promotions have significantly boosted Google Pay's transaction volumes during peak periods. By associating digital payments with festive shopping and gifting, Google Pay has ingrained itself into the cultural fabric of financial transactions in India.

PayPal: Comprehensive Social Media Strategy

PayPal, one of the oldest and most established digital payment platforms, employs a comprehensive social media strategy to maintain its market position and attract new users.

Educational and Promotional Content

PayPal frequently posts educational content on its social media channels, including tips for secure online shopping, how-to guides for using PayPal services, and updates on new features. Promotional content includes special offers and discounts for users who make purchases with PayPal.

Impact: PayPal's consistent educational and promotional efforts on social media have helped reinforce its brand as a trusted and secure payment platform. According to **Statista** (2021), PayPal had 392 million active accounts worldwide, highlighting the effectiveness of its social media strategy in maintaining and growing its user base.

PayPal Community Forum

PayPal also engages with its users through the PayPal Community Forum, where users can ask questions, share experiences, and provide feedback. This forum is promoted across PayPal's social media channels, driving traffic and engagement.

Impact: The community forum has created a space for users to connect and support each other, fostering loyalty and trust. By promoting this forum on social media, PayPal has enhanced its customer support capabilities and strengthened its user community.

Chapter 6

Security and Privacy Concerns

As digital wallets and payment apps become increasingly prevalent in financial transactions, the need for robust security measures has grown correspondingly. These platforms handle sensitive financial information and must ensure the safety and privacy of their users. This section explores the common security features integrated into digital wallets and payment apps to protect user data and transactions.

Encryption

Encryption is a fundamental security feature used by digital wallets and payment apps to protect data. Encryption transforms data into a coded format that can only be deciphered by authorized parties with the correct decryption key.

End-to-End Encryption: This method ensures that data is encrypted on the sender's device and only decrypted on the recipient's device, preventing unauthorized access during transmission. Platforms like **Apple Pay** and **Google Pay** use end-to-end encryption to secure payment information and transactions.

Data Storage Encryption: Digital wallets often encrypt data stored on devices or servers. For example, **PayPal** employs strong encryption to protect user data both in transit and at rest, ensuring that personal and financial information remains secure even if the data is intercepted or accessed by unauthorized entities.

Tokenization

Tokenization replaces sensitive data, such as credit card numbers, with a unique identifier called a token. This token is useless if intercepted, as it cannot be reverse-engineered to reveal the original data.

Apple Pay and **Google Pay** are prominent users of tokenization. When a transaction is made, these platforms generate a one-time token that is sent to the merchant instead of the actual card number. This reduces the risk of card information being stolen during transactions.

Biometric Authentication

Biometric authentication adds an extra layer of security by requiring a physical characteristic unique to the user for verification. Common biometric methods include fingerprint scanning, facial recognition, and iris scanning.

Fingerprint Scanning: Used by apps like **Venmo** and **Cash App**, fingerprint scanning ensures that only the registered user can access the app or authorize transactions.

Facial Recognition: **Apple Pay** employs Face ID, which scans the user's face to authenticate payments. This method is highly secure as it uses advanced algorithms to recognize facial features and is difficult to spoof.

Iris Scanning: Some Android devices equipped with iris

scanners can use this feature for authentication in apps like **Samsung Pay**. Iris scanning is highly accurate and provides an additional security measure.

Multi-Factor Authentication (MFA)

Multi-factor authentication requires users to provide two or more verification factors to gain access to their accounts. This typically involves something the user knows (a password), something the user has (a smartphone or hardware token), and something the user is (biometric verification).

PayPal and **Google Pay** both utilize MFA to enhance security. For example, a user may be required to enter a password and then verify a one-time code sent to their phone. This makes it significantly harder for unauthorized users to gain access, even if they have the password.

Secure Element Technology

Secure Element (SE) is a dedicated chip in devices that securely stores sensitive information, such as payment data and cryptographic keys. This technology is isolated from the main operating system, making it resistant to malware and unauthorized access.

Apple Pay and **Samsung Pay** use secure element technology to store payment information. When a transaction is made, the secure element handles the payment data securely, ensuring that the main operating system does not have direct access to sensitive information.

Real-Time Fraud Monitoring

Real-time fraud monitoring involves continuously analyzing transactions for suspicious activity. Advanced algorithms and machine learning models are used to detect anomalies and potential fraudulent behavior.

Cash App and **PayPal** employ real-time fraud monitoring systems. These systems flag unusual transactions, such as large withdrawals or transfers from unfamiliar locations, and can prompt users for additional verification or temporarily freeze accounts to prevent unauthorized activity.

Secure Sockets Layer (SSL) and Transport Layer Security (TLS)

SSL and TLS are cryptographic protocols designed to provide secure communication over a computer network. These protocols are used to encrypt data transmitted between users and servers, ensuring that sensitive information is not exposed to eavesdroppers.

Most digital wallets and payment apps, including **Venmo** and **Google Pay**, use SSL/TLS to secure the data transmitted during transactions. This encryption helps protect against man-in-the-middle attacks, where an attacker intercepts and potentially alters the communication between two parties.

Regular Security Audits and Updates

Regular security audits and updates are critical to maintaining the security of digital wallets and payment apps. These audits involve thorough examinations of the platform's code, infrastructure, and security protocols to identify and address vulnerabilities.

Apple Pay, **Google Pay**, and **PayPal** routinely perform security audits and release updates to fix any identified security issues. By staying proactive about security, these platforms can protect against emerging threats and vulnerabilities.

User Education and Awareness

Educating users about security best practices is an essential component of protecting digital wallets and payment apps. Many platforms provide resources and tips to help users understand how to secure their accounts and recognize potential threats.

PayPal offers comprehensive security guidance on its website, advising users to enable MFA, recognize phishing attempts, and regularly review their account activity. By promoting user awareness, digital wallet companies can reduce the risk of user errors that could compromise security.

Regulatory Compliance

Compliance with industry standards and regulations is crucial for ensuring the security of digital wallets and payment apps. Regulations such as the Payment Card Industry Data Security Standard (PCI DSS) and the General Data Protection Regulation (GDPR) set strict requirements for the protection of payment and personal data.

Venmo, **Cash App**, and **Google Pay** adhere to PCI DSS guidelines, ensuring that they meet the highest standards for secure payment processing. Compliance with GDPR is also important, particularly for platforms operating in Europe, as it mandates stringent data protection measures and user privacy rights.

Privacy Issues and Data Protection Measures in Digital Wallets and Payment Apps

Digital wallets and payment apps have revolutionized the way people manage their finances, offering unparalleled convenience and accessibility. However, these benefits come with significant privacy issues and data protection concerns. This section examines the primary privacy issues associated with digital wallets and payment apps and explores the data protection measures that companies implement to safeguard user information.

Privacy Issues in Digital Wallets and Payment Apps
Data Collection and Usage

Digital wallets and payment apps collect vast amounts of personal and financial data, including transaction histories, location data, and personal identifiers. While this data is necessary for the functionality of the apps, it raises privacy concerns regarding how this information is used and stored.

For instance, **Venmo** and **PayPal** collect data to provide personalized services and improve user experience. However, users often worry about the extent of data collection and potential misuse. According to a **Pew Research Center** report (2019), 79% of Americans are concerned about how companies use their data.

Data Sharing with Third Parties

Another significant privacy issue is the sharing of user data with third parties. Digital wallet providers may share data with affiliates, advertisers, and other business partners for various purposes, including marketing and analytics. This practice can lead to privacy breaches if third parties do not adhere to stringent data protection standards.

Google Pay and **Apple Pay**, for example, have faced scrutiny over their data sharing practices. While both companies emphasize their commitment to user privacy, the involvement of multiple stakeholders in data processing increases the risk of data exposure.

Security Breaches and Cyber Attacks

Security breaches and cyber attacks pose a direct threat to the privacy of digital wallet users. Cybercriminals target these platforms to steal sensitive data, which can then be used for identity theft, financial fraud, and other malicious activities.

Cash App experienced a significant breach in 2022 when a former employee accessed customer data, highlighting the vulnerability of digital wallets to insider threats. Such incidents underscore the importance of robust security measures to protect user privacy.

Data Protection Measures in Digital Wallets and Payment Apps

Encryption

Encryption is a critical data protection measure used to safeguard user information. It involves converting data into a coded format that can only be deciphered with a specific key, making it unreadable to unauthorized users.

End-to-End Encryption: Both **Apple Pay** and **Google Pay** use end-to-end encryption to protect data during transmission. This ensures that sensitive information remains confidential and secure from the point of entry to the recipient.

Data Storage Encryption: Digital wallets like **Venmo** and **PayPal** employ encryption for data stored on their servers. This measure protects user information from unauthorized access even if the data is intercepted or the servers are compromised.

Tokenization

Tokenization replaces sensitive data, such as credit card numbers, with unique tokens. These tokens can be used for transactions but have no exploitable value if intercepted.

Apple Pay and **Google Pay** use tokenization extensively. When a user makes a transaction, the actual card details are not shared with the merchant. Instead, a token is used to process the payment, significantly reducing the risk of data theft.

Biometric Authentication

Biometric authentication adds an additional layer of security by requiring unique physical characteristics for access. Common methods include fingerprint scanning and facial recognition.

Fingerprint Scanning: Used by apps like **Venmo** and **Cash App**, fingerprint scanning ensures that only the authorized user can access the app and authorize transactions.

Facial Recognition: **Apple Pay** employs Face ID technology, which scans the user's face to authenticate payments. This method is highly secure and difficult to spoof.

Multi-Factor Authentication (MFA)

MFA enhances security by requiring multiple forms of verification before granting access. This typically involves something the user knows (password), something the user has (smartphone or hardware token), and something the user is (biometric data).

PayPal and **Google Pay** use MFA to add an extra layer of security. For instance, users might be required to enter a password and then verify a code sent to their phone, making unauthorized access much more difficult.

Secure Sockets Layer (SSL) and Transport Layer Security (TLS)

SSL and TLS are cryptographic protocols that provide secure communication over a network. They encrypt the data transmitted between users and servers, protecting it from eavesdropping and tampering.

Most digital wallets, including **Apple Pay** and **Venmo**, use SSL/TLS to secure data transmission. This ensures that sensitive information, such as payment details and personal data, remains protected during transit.

Regular Security Audits and Updates

Regular security audits and updates are essential for maintaining the security and privacy of digital wallets. These audits involve thorough examinations of the platform's code, infrastructure, and security protocols to identify and address vulnerabilities.

Apple Pay, **Google Pay**, and **PayPal** conduct frequent security audits and release updates to patch any identified security issues. This proactive approach helps to protect against emerging threats and vulnerabilities.

Compliance with Regulations

Adhering to industry standards and regulations is crucial for ensuring the privacy and security of user data. Regulations like the General Data Protection Regulation (GDPR) and the Payment Card Industry Data Security Standard (PCI DSS) set stringent requirements for data protection.

Apple Pay, **Venmo**, and **Cash App** comply with PCI DSS guidelines, ensuring that they meet high standards for secure payment processing. GDPR compliance is particularly important for platforms operating in Europe, as it mandates rigorous data protection measures and user privacy rights.

Transparency and User Control

Providing transparency and control over personal data is a key aspect of privacy protection. Digital wallet providers should offer clear information about data collection practices and give users the ability to manage their data.

Google Pay and **Apple Pay** allow users to review and manage their privacy settings. Users can control what data is collected, how it is used, and with whom it is shared. This transparency helps build trust and empowers users to take charge of their privacy.

How Gen Alpha and Gen Z Perceive and Handle Security Concerns

The rise of digital technologies has significantly influenced the behavior and attitudes of Generation Alpha (born from 2010 onwards) and Generation Z (born from 1997 to 2012). These generations have grown up in an era where digital interactions are the norm, shaping their perceptions of security and privacy. Understanding how these young cohorts perceive and handle security concerns is crucial for developing effective strategies to protect their digital lives. This section explores the attitudes, behaviors, and strategies of Gen Alpha and Gen Z regarding security concerns, supported by data and research.

Perception of Security Concerns

Gen Z's Digital Savviness

Generation Z is the first generation to grow up with smartphones and social media, making them highly digitally savvy. Their familiarity with technology influences their perception of security. According to a report by **Pew Research Center** (2018), 45% of teens report being online "almost constantly," which makes them acutely aware of digital security threats.

Gen Z is particularly concerned about the security of their personal information. They are aware of the risks associated with data breaches and identity theft, having witnessed several high-profile incidents in their lifetime. This generation values transparency and often scrutinizes the privacy policies of the apps and services they use.

Gen Alpha's Early Exposure

Generation Alpha, currently in their early childhood and adolescence, is growing up with even more advanced technology, including artificial intelligence and the Internet of Things (IoT). Their exposure to technology from a very young age shapes their understanding and approach to security.

While concrete data on Gen Alpha's attitudes is still emerging, early indications suggest that they will likely inherit and amplify Gen Z's concerns about privacy and security. The educational environment and parental influence play significant roles in shaping their perception of security. Schools and parents are increasingly incorporating digital literacy and cybersecurity education into early learning curriculums, emphasizing the importance of protecting personal information online.

Both Gen Z and Gen Alpha are more proactive in handling security concerns compared to previous generations. They are more likely to use advanced security measures such as biometric authentication, multi-factor authentication (MFA), and password managers.

Biometric Authentication: Gen Z, in particular, is comfortable using biometric authentication methods like fingerprint scanning and facial recognition. According to a **Statista** report (2020), 78% of Gen Z respondents prefer biometric authentication over traditional passwords for its convenience and security.

Multi-Factor Authentication: MFA is widely adopted among these generations. They understand the importance of adding an extra layer of security to their accounts. A survey by **Microsoft** (2019) found that 86% of Gen Z users enabled MFA on their accounts, indicating a strong preference for this security measure.

Password Managers: Using password managers is another common practice. These tools generate and store strong, unique passwords for different accounts, reducing the risk of password-related breaches. The same **Microsoft** survey reported that 65% of Gen Z users utilize password managers to secure their digital identities.

Awareness and Education

Education plays a pivotal role in shaping how Gen Alpha and Gen Z handle security concerns. Schools and organizations are increasingly offering digital literacy programs that include cybersecurity education. These programs teach students about the risks of sharing personal information online, recognizing phishing attempts, and the importance of maintaining strong, unique passwords.

Parental Guidance: For Gen Alpha, parental guidance is crucial. Parents who are aware of digital risks often implement security measures on devices used by their children. Tools such as parental controls, monitoring software, and restricted access to certain websites help protect younger users from potential threats.

Educational Initiatives: Initiatives like Google's **Be Internet Awesome** and Microsoft's **Digital Civility Index** aim to educate young users about online safety. These programs provide resources and interactive activities to help children and teens understand the importance of protecting their personal information and recognizing online threats.

Use of Privacy-Focused Apps and Services

Both generations show a preference for apps and services that prioritize privacy and security. They are more likely to choose platforms that offer robust privacy features and transparent data usage policies.

Privacy-Focused Platforms: Apps like **Signal** and **Telegram**, known for their strong encryption and privacy features, are gaining popularity among these groups. According to a report by **App Annie** (2021), there was a significant increase in downloads of privacy-focused messaging apps among young users following high-profile data breaches and changes in privacy policies by mainstream platforms.

Data Minimization: Gen Z, in particular, appreciates platforms that practice data minimization—collecting only the data necessary for the service to function. They are cautious about granting permissions and are more likely to opt out of data collection when given the choice.

Challenges and Concerns

Data Breaches and Trust Issues

Despite their proactive approach, Gen Alpha and Gen Z face challenges related to trust in digital platforms. High-profile data breaches and controversies over data misuse by major companies have eroded trust. According to a **Pew Research Center** report (2019), 70% of Gen Z respondents expressed concerns about their data being used in ways they did not expect.

Overconfidence and Security Fatigue

Another challenge is the potential for overconfidence and security fatigue. Gen Z, being highly tech-savvy, might underestimate certain risks or become desensitized to security warnings due to their frequency. Security fatigue can lead to lax security practices, such as reusing passwords or ignoring software updates, which can compromise their digital security.

7

Chapter 7

Chapter 6: Financial Literacy and Digital Payments

The Importance of Financial Education for Younger Generations

Financial education is increasingly recognized as a critical component of personal development, especially for younger generations such as Gen Z and Gen Alpha. As these cohorts enter an increasingly complex financial landscape, equipped with advanced technology and diverse financial products, the need for comprehensive financial education has never been more urgent. This section explores the importance of financial education for younger generations, examining the benefits, current gaps, and strategies for effective financial literacy programs.

Benefits of Financial Education
Enhanced Financial Decision-Making
Financial education equips young people with the knowledge

and skills necessary to make informed financial decisions. Understanding basic concepts such as budgeting, saving, investing, and managing debt can significantly impact their financial well-being.

A study by the **FINRA Investor Education Foundation** (2018) found that individuals with higher financial literacy are more likely to plan for retirement and have an emergency fund. These behaviors are critical for long-term financial stability and security.

Reducing Financial Anxiety

Financial literacy can also help reduce financial anxiety and stress. Many young people experience stress related to money management, which can affect their mental health and overall well-being. Educating them about financial management can alleviate these concerns by providing them with the confidence and competence to handle their finances effectively.

According to a survey by **The National Endowment for Financial Education** (2019), 88% of respondents who had taken a financial education course reported feeling less stressed about money.

Promoting Responsible Financial Behaviors

Financial education fosters responsible financial behaviors from an early age. By learning the value of money and the importance of saving and investing, young people are more likely to develop habits that lead to financial success.

Research by **Jump$tart Coalition** (2020) indicates that students who receive financial education are more likely to display positive financial behaviors, such as budgeting, saving regularly, and avoiding unnecessary debt.

Current Gaps in Financial Education

Despite the clear benefits, there are significant gaps in financial education across various educational systems. Many young people lack the essential financial knowledge required to navigate today's complex financial world.

Inconsistent Financial Education Programs

The availability and quality of financial education programs vary widely. Some schools offer comprehensive courses, while others provide little to no financial education. This inconsistency leaves many students without the necessary knowledge to manage their finances effectively.

According to the **Council for Economic Education** (2020), only 21 states in the U.S. require high school students to take a course in personal finance. This leaves a significant portion of the student population without formal financial education.

Socioeconomic Disparities

Socioeconomic disparities also play a role in access to financial education. Students from lower-income families are less likely to receive financial education at home and may attend schools that do not offer such programs. This disparity can lead to long-term financial inequality.

A report by the **Consumer Financial Protection Bureau** (2019) highlighted that students from lower-income families are at a higher risk of financial instability and can greatly benefit from targeted financial education programs.

Lack of Teacher Training

Another gap in financial education is the lack of teacher training. Many educators do not feel confident teaching financial literacy due to their own lack of knowledge and resources. This issue hinders the effectiveness of financial education programs.

The **National Financial Educators Council** (2020) found that 89% of teachers believe that financial education is important, but only 20% feel very confident in their ability to teach it.

Strategies for Effective Financial Education

To address these gaps and enhance financial education for younger generations, several strategies can be implemented.

Integrating Financial Education into School Curriculums

One of the most effective ways to improve financial literacy is to integrate financial education into the standard school curriculum. This ensures that all students receive a basic understanding of financial concepts before they graduate.

States like Florida and Virginia have mandated personal finance courses for high school students, setting a precedent for other states to follow. Research from the **University of Wisconsin-Madison** (2019) shows that students who take personal finance courses in high school are more likely to make informed financial decisions as adults.

Providing Teacher Training and Resources

Equipping teachers with the necessary knowledge and resources is crucial for the success of financial education programs. Professional development workshops and comprehensive teaching materials can help educators feel more confident in delivering financial literacy lessons.

Organizations like **Next Gen Personal Finance** offer free resources and training for teachers, helping to bridge the gap in financial education.

Utilizing Technology and Interactive Tools

Leveraging technology can enhance the effectiveness of financial education. Interactive tools, such as online courses, mobile apps, and simulation games, can make learning about finance engaging and accessible for young people.

Platforms like **Khan Academy** and **EverFi** provide interactive financial education modules that cover a wide range of topics, from basic budgeting to investing. These tools cater to different learning styles and can be accessed anytime, making financial education more flexible and inclusive.

Promoting Financial Education at Home

Parents and guardians play a crucial role in their children's financial education. Encouraging discussions about money, involving children in budgeting and shopping, and providing allowances linked to chores can teach valuable financial lessons.

A survey by **T. Rowe Price** (2020) found that children who discuss money with their parents are more likely to develop positive financial habits. Parental involvement can reinforce the lessons learned at school and provide practical, real-world experience.

Implementing Community-Based Programs

Community-based financial education programs can reach students who may not receive adequate financial education at school. These programs can be offered through local organizations, libraries, and youth groups.

For example, **Junior Achievement USA** offers programs that teach financial literacy, work readiness, and entrepreneurship to students across the country. These initiatives can supplement school-based education and provide additional support for students.

Resources and Tools for Improving Financial Literacy

Financial literacy is a crucial skill that enables individuals to make informed decisions about their finances. As the financial landscape becomes increasingly complex, it is essential to equip people, especially the younger generations, with the necessary knowledge and skills. There are numerous resources and tools available that can significantly improve financial literacy. This section explores various platforms, programs, and initiatives designed to enhance financial education for individuals of all ages.

Online Courses and Educational Platforms

Online courses and educational platforms offer structured and comprehensive learning experiences for those seeking to improve their financial literacy. These resources often include interactive content, quizzes, and real-world scenarios to help users apply their knowledge.

Khan Academy

Khan Academy is a widely recognized educational platform that offers a variety of free courses on personal finance. Topics range from saving and budgeting to investing and retirement planning. The courses are designed to be accessible to learners of all ages and educational backgrounds.

Impact: Khan Academy's comprehensive approach to financial education helps users build a solid foundation in personal finance, making complex topics more understandable and manageable.

Coursera and edX

Coursera and **edX** are online learning platforms that provide access to courses from top universities and institutions. They offer numerous financial literacy courses, including "Financial Markets" by Yale University and "Personal Finance" by the University of Florida.

Impact: These platforms provide high-quality education from reputable institutions, allowing learners to gain in-depth knowledge from experts in the field. The flexibility of online learning enables individuals to study at their own pace.

Mobile Apps

Mobile apps are convenient tools for improving financial

literacy, offering on-the-go learning and real-time financial management capabilities. These apps often include budgeting tools, financial calculators, and educational content.

Mint is a popular budgeting app that helps users track their spending, set financial goals, and manage their finances. The app provides personalized tips and insights based on users' financial behaviors.

Impact: Mint's user-friendly interface and comprehensive features make it easier for individuals to understand and manage their finances, promoting better financial habits.

YNAB is a budgeting app that focuses on helping users allocate every dollar they earn. The app offers educational content and workshops to teach users about budgeting, saving, and managing debt.

Impact: YNAB's hands-on approach to budgeting encourages users to be proactive with their finances, fostering long-term financial stability and literacy.

Acorns is an investment app that helps users invest spare change from everyday purchases. The app also offers educational content through its "Grow" magazine, which covers topics related to saving, investing, and financial planning.

Impact: Acorns makes investing accessible to beginners, helping users understand the importance of investing and how to start building wealth with small amounts of money.

Interactive Tools and Simulations

Interactive tools and simulations provide practical experiences that enhance financial literacy by allowing users to apply their knowledge in simulated environments.

Financial Football, developed by Visa, is an interactive game that teaches financial concepts through a virtual football game. Players answer financial questions to advance down the field and score touchdowns.

Impact: This engaging approach to financial education makes learning fun and interactive, helping users retain information and apply it in real-life situations.

Budget Challenge is a simulation game that provides a hands-on experience in managing a budget. Users navigate various financial scenarios, such as paying bills, managing debt, and saving for emergencies.

Impact: By simulating real-life financial decisions, Budget Challenge helps users understand the consequences of their choices and develop practical money management skills.

Community programs and workshops offer personalized financial education and support, often provided by local organizations, non-profits, and financial institutions.

Junior Achievement USA offers programs that teach financial literacy, work readiness, and entrepreneurship to students from kindergarten through high school. Their programs include classroom activities, after-school programs, and experiential learning opportunities.

Impact: Junior Achievement's comprehensive approach helps students develop essential financial skills from a young age, preparing them for future financial success.

The **National Endowment for Financial Education** provides a variety of resources and programs aimed at improving financial literacy. NEFE offers workshops, online courses, and educational materials covering topics such as budgeting, credit management, and retirement planning.

Impact: NEFE's resources reach a wide audience, including educators, students, and adults, helping to improve financial literacy across different demographics.

Many local credit unions and banks offer financial literacy workshops and seminars for their members. These sessions cover various topics, including budgeting, credit management, home buying, and retirement planning.

Impact: Financial institutions provide valuable, community-based resources that address the specific needs and challenges of their members, fostering better financial literacy at a local level.

Government agencies and non-profit organizations play a crucial role in promoting financial literacy through various programs and initiatives.

Consumer Financial Protection Bureau (CFPB)

The **Consumer Financial Protection Bureau** offers numerous resources to help consumers understand and manage their finances. Their tools include budgeting worksheets, credit score information, and debt management guides.

Impact: The CFPB's resources are designed to empower consumers with the knowledge and skills needed to make informed financial decisions, promoting financial stability and protection.

Jump$tart Coalition for Personal Financial Literacy

The **Jump$tart Coalition** is a non-profit organization that advocates for effective financial education in schools. They provide resources, standards, and support for educators to implement financial literacy programs.

Impact: By focusing on educational reform, Jump$tart Coalition helps ensure that financial literacy is integrated into school curriculums, reaching students at a critical stage in their development.

Federal Trade Commission (FTC)

The **Federal Trade Commission** offers resources and tools to help consumers protect themselves from fraud and scams. Their website provides information on identity theft, credit, and consumer rights.

Impact: The FTC's resources help individuals understand and navigate the financial risks they may encounter, promoting informed and cautious financial behaviors.

Impact of Digital Payments on Financial Habits and Understanding

The proliferation of digital payments has significantly transformed financial habits and understanding among consumers. Digital payment platforms like **Venmo**, **Cash App**, **Apple Pay**, and others have made financial transactions more accessible, convenient, and instantaneous. This section examines how digital payments have impacted consumer financial behaviors, enhanced financial literacy, and altered the landscape of financial interactions.

Increased Convenience and Accessibility

Instantaneous Transactions

Digital payment platforms have revolutionized the speed of financial transactions. Traditional methods, such as checks and bank transfers, often involve delays, whereas digital payments enable instant money transfers. This immediacy caters to the modern consumer's demand for speed and efficiency.

For instance, **Venmo** and **Cash App** allow users to transfer money to friends and family within seconds. The convenience of instant payments is particularly beneficial for splitting bills, paying rent, or making quick payments in social settings. According to a report by **Statista** (2021), mobile payment transactions in the United States are projected to exceed $700 billion by 2023, underscoring the growing preference for digital payment solutions.

Accessibility for the Unbanked

Digital payments have also increased financial accessibility for unbanked and underbanked populations. Mobile payment platforms provide an entry point into the financial system for individuals who may not have access to traditional banking services.

PayPal and **Google Pay** offer services that require only a smartphone and internet connection, enabling users to participate in the digital economy without needing a traditional bank account. The **World Bank** (2018) reported that digital financial services have helped increase financial inclusion, particularly in developing countries where banking infrastructure is limited.

Enhanced Financial Literacy and Awareness

Real-Time Financial Tracking

One of the most significant impacts of digital payments is the enhancement of financial literacy through real-time tracking and management tools. Digital payment platforms often include features that help users monitor their spending and manage their finances more effectively.

Mint, a popular budgeting app, aggregates data from various financial accounts to provide users with a comprehensive view of their finances. By categorizing transactions and offering insights into spending habits, Mint helps users make informed financial decisions. According to **NerdWallet** (2020), users who actively track their spending are more likely to stick to their budgets and achieve their financial goals.

Financial Education through Apps

Digital payment platforms often include educational components to improve users' financial literacy. Apps like **Acorns** and **Stash** not only facilitate investments but also provide educational content to help users understand financial concepts and investment strategies.

Acorns offers a feature called "Grow," which includes sections, videos, and tutorials on personal finance topics. This educational approach helps users develop a better understanding of financial planning and investment, fostering long-term financial health.

Behavioral Changes and Financial Habits

Encouragement of Saving and Investing

Digital payment platforms have made saving and investing more accessible and engaging. Features like round-up savings and micro-investing encourage users to save and invest small amounts regularly, making these activities a part of daily financial habits.

Acorns automatically rounds up users' purchases to the nearest dollar and invests the spare change into diversified portfolios. This "set it and forget it" approach lowers the barrier to entry for investing and encourages consistent saving. A study by **The National Bureau of Economic Research** (2019) found that users of automated savings tools are more likely to build substantial savings over time compared to those who rely solely on manual methods.

Increased Financial Discipline

The transparency and instant feedback provided by digital payment platforms promote increased financial discipline among users. By offering real-time notifications and detailed transaction histories, these platforms help users stay on top of their finances and avoid overspending.

YNAB (You Need A Budget) is an app that emphasizes proactive budgeting, requiring users to allocate every dollar they earn. This approach encourages users to think critically about their spending and prioritize their financial goals, leading to more disciplined financial behaviors.

Privacy and Security Considerations

Enhanced Security Features

Digital payment platforms have implemented robust security measures to protect users' financial information. Features such as encryption, tokenization, and biometric authentication enhance the security of transactions and reduce the risk of fraud.

Apple Pay uses tokenization to replace sensitive card information with a unique identifier, making transactions more secure. Additionally, biometric authentication methods like Face ID and Touch ID provide an extra layer of security, ensuring that only authorized users can initiate transactions.

Privacy Concerns

Despite the enhanced security features, digital payments also raise privacy concerns. The collection and storage of personal and financial data by digital payment platforms can be a point of vulnerability. Users need to be aware of how their data is being used and take steps to protect their privacy.

According to a **Pew Research Center** report (2019), 79% of Americans are concerned about how companies use their data. Digital payment platforms must prioritize transparency and user control over data to build trust and ensure the protection of user privacy.

Implications for Financial Institutions

Disruption of Traditional Banking

The rise of digital payments has disrupted traditional banking models, forcing financial institutions to adapt to changing consumer preferences. Banks are increasingly integrating digital payment solutions into their services to remain competitive.

Chase QuickPay with Zelle and **Bank of America's partnership with Zelle** are examples of traditional banks adopting digital payment technologies to offer customers the convenience and speed they expect. These integrations help banks retain customers who might otherwise turn to standalone digital payment platforms.

Opportunities for Innovation

The digital payment landscape also presents opportunities for financial innovation. Fintech companies and traditional financial institutions can collaborate to develop new products and services that meet evolving consumer needs.

For instance, **Venmo**'s partnership with Mastercard to offer a Venmo debit card and **Square's Cash App** integration with Bitcoin trading demonstrate how digital payment platforms can innovate and expand their offerings. These innovations not only enhance user experience but also create new revenue streams for financial institutions.

CHAPTER 7

Impact of Digital Payments on Financial Habits and Understanding, with a Focus on Accessibility for the Unbanked

The proliferation of digital payments has significantly transformed financial habits and understanding among consumers. Digital payment platforms like **Venmo**, **Cash App**, **Apple Pay**, and others have made financial transactions more accessible, convenient, and instantaneous. This section examines how digital payments have impacted consumer financial behaviors, enhanced financial literacy, and altered the landscape of financial interactions, with a particular focus on how these platforms have increased accessibility for unbanked and underbanked populations.

Increased Convenience and Accessibility

Instantaneous Transactions

Digital payment platforms have revolutionized the speed of financial transactions. Traditional methods, such as checks and bank transfers, often involve delays, whereas digital payments enable instant money transfers. This immediacy caters to the modern consumer's demand for speed and efficiency.

For instance, **Venmo** and **Cash App** allow users to transfer money to friends and family within seconds. The convenience of instant payments is particularly beneficial for splitting bills, paying rent, or making quick payments in social settings. According to a report by **Statista** (2021), mobile payment transactions in the United States are projected to exceed $700 billion by 2023, underscoring the growing preference for digital payment solutions.

Accessibility for the Unbanked

Digital payments have significantly increased financial accessibility for unbanked and underbanked populations. Traditional banking services are often out of reach for many due to geographic, economic, or systemic barriers. However, digital payment platforms have provided an entry point into the financial system for these individuals, offering essential financial services through smartphones and internet connections.

PayPal and **Google Pay** offer services that require only a smartphone and internet connection, enabling users to participate in the digital economy without needing a traditional bank account. These platforms offer an array of services, including sending and receiving money, making online purchases, and even paying bills.

A report by the **World Bank** (2018) highlighted that digital financial services have been instrumental in increasing financial inclusion, particularly in developing countries. For instance, in Sub-Saharan Africa, mobile money services have provided financial access to millions who previously had no access to formal financial systems. According to the report, the percentage of adults with a mobile money account in Sub-Saharan Africa grew from 12% in 2014 to 21% in 2017.

Bridging the Gap with Mobile Money Services

Mobile money services have played a crucial role in bridging the financial inclusion gap for the unbanked. These services allow users to store money, send and receive payments, and conduct other financial transactions using their mobile phones. Examples of successful mobile money services include **M-Pesa** in Kenya, **GCash** in the Philippines, and **bKash** in Bangladesh.

M-Pesa has been particularly impactful, transforming the financial landscape in Kenya. Launched in 2007, M-Pesa enables users to deposit, withdraw, transfer money, and pay for goods and services using a simple text message system. As of 2020, M-Pesa had over 41 million users in Kenya alone, with the service expanding to other countries in Africa, Asia, and Eastern Europe.

Financial Inclusion in Developed Countries

Even in developed countries, digital payment platforms have improved financial inclusion for unbanked and underbanked populations. In the United States, an estimated 6% of households were unbanked in 2019, according to the **Federal Deposit Insurance Corporation (FDIC)**. Digital payment platforms like **Cash App** and **PayPal** provide these individuals with access to essential financial services without the need for a traditional bank account.

Cash App offers features such as direct deposits, bill payments, and the ability to buy and sell Bitcoin, all accessible via a mobile app. These services enable users to manage their finances more effectively and participate in the digital economy, reducing their reliance on cash and informal financial systems.

Enhanced Financial Literacy and Awareness

Real-Time Financial Tracking

One of the most significant impacts of digital payments is the enhancement of financial literacy through real-time tracking and management tools. Digital payment platforms often include features that help users monitor their spending and manage their finances more effectively.

Mint, a popular budgeting app, aggregates data from various financial accounts to provide users with a comprehensive view of their finances. By categorizing transactions and offering insights into spending habits, Mint helps users make informed financial decisions. According to **NerdWallet** (2020), users who actively track their spending are more likely to stick to their budgets and achieve their financial goals.

Financial Education through Apps

Digital payment platforms often include educational components to improve users' financial literacy. Apps like **Acorns** and **Stash** not only facilitate investments but also provide educational content to help users understand financial concepts and investment strategies.

Acorns offers a feature called "Grow," which includes sections, videos, and tutorials on personal finance topics. This educational approach helps users develop a better understanding of financial planning and investment, fostering long-term financial health.

Behavioral Changes and Financial Habits
Encouragement of Saving and Investing

Digital payment platforms have made saving and investing more accessible and engaging. Features like round-up savings and micro-investing encourage users to save and invest small amounts regularly, making these activities a part of daily financial habits.

Acorns automatically rounds up users' purchases to the nearest dollar and invests the spare change into diversified portfolios. This "set it and forget it" approach lowers the barrier to entry for investing and encourages consistent saving. A study by **The National Bureau of Economic Research** (2019) found that users of automated savings tools are more likely to build substantial savings over time compared to those who rely solely on manual methods.

Increased Financial Discipline

The transparency and instant feedback provided by digital payment platforms promote increased financial discipline among users. By offering real-time notifications and detailed transaction histories, these platforms help users stay on top of their finances and avoid overspending.

YNAB (You Need A Budget) is an app that emphasizes proactive budgeting, requiring users to allocate every dollar they earn. This approach encourages users to think critically about their spending and prioritize their financial goals, leading to more disciplined financial behaviors.

Privacy and Security Considerations

Enhanced Security Features

Digital payment platforms have implemented robust security measures to protect users' financial information. Features such as encryption, tokenization, and biometric authentication enhance the security of transactions and reduce the risk of fraud.

Apple Pay uses tokenization to replace sensitive card information with a unique identifier, making transactions more secure. Additionally, biometric authentication methods like Face ID and Touch ID provide an extra layer of security, ensuring that only authorized users can initiate transactions.

Privacy Concerns

Despite the enhanced security features, digital payments also raise privacy concerns. The collection and storage of personal and financial data by digital payment platforms can be a point of vulnerability. Users need to be aware of how their data is being used and take steps to protect their privacy.

According to a **Pew Research Center** report (2019), 79% of Americans are concerned about how companies use their data. Digital payment platforms must prioritize transparency and user control over data to build trust and ensure the protection of user privacy.

Implications for Financial Institutions

Disruption of Traditional Banking

The rise of digital payments has disrupted traditional banking models, forcing financial institutions to adapt to changing consumer preferences. Banks are increasingly integrating digital payment solutions into their services to remain competitive.

Chase QuickPay with Zelle and **Bank of America's partnership with Zelle** are examples of traditional banks adopting digital payment technologies to offer customers the convenience and speed they expect. These integrations help banks retain customers who might otherwise turn to standalone digital payment platforms.

Opportunities for Innovation

The digital payment landscape also presents opportunities for financial innovation. Fintech companies and traditional financial institutions can collaborate to develop new products and services that meet evolving consumer needs.

For instance, **Venmo**'s partnership with Mastercard to offer a Venmo debit card and **Square's Cash App** integration with Bitcoin trading demonstrate how digital payment platforms can innovate and expand their offerings. These innovations not only enhance user experience but also create new revenue streams for financial institutions.

8

Chapter 8

Chapter 7: The Future of Cashless Transactions

Trends and Predictions for the Future of Digital Payments

The landscape of digital payments has evolved rapidly over the past decade, driven by technological advancements, changing consumer behaviors, and increased financial inclusion. As we look to the future, several key trends and predictions are expected to shape the evolution of digital payments. This section explores these trends and provides insights into the future of digital financial transactions.

Trends Shaping the Future of Digital Payments

Increased Adoption of Contactless Payments

The COVID-19 pandemic significantly accelerated the adoption of contactless payments as consumers sought safer, more hygienic ways to transact. This trend is expected to continue growing, driven by convenience, speed, and security.

NFC Technology: Near Field Communication (NFC) technology, which enables contactless payments, is becoming standard in smartphones and payment terminals. According to **Juniper Research** (2021), contactless payment transactions are projected to reach $6 trillion globally by 2024, up from $2 trillion in 2020.

Wearable Devices: The use of wearable devices like smartwatches for contactless payments is also on the rise. Devices from brands like **Apple**, **Samsung**, and **Garmin** are integrating payment capabilities, allowing users to make transactions without reaching for their wallets or phones.

Growth of Digital Wallets

Digital wallets are becoming the preferred method for managing finances and making payments, offering a convenient way to store and use multiple payment methods securely.

Comprehensive Financial Management: Digital wallets like **PayPal**, **Apple Pay**, and **Google Pay** are expanding their functionalities beyond payments to include budgeting tools, loyalty programs, and investment options. This trend towards "super apps" is creating all-in-one financial platforms that cater to a wide range of consumer needs.

Cryptocurrency Integration: As cryptocurrencies gain mainstream acceptance, digital wallets are integrating the ability to buy, sell, and hold cryptocurrencies. **Cash App** and **PayPal** already offer these services, and more digital wallets are expected to follow suit. A report by **Statista** (2021) indicates that the number of cryptocurrency wallet users worldwide reached over 70 million by the end of 2021, and this number is expected to grow as digital wallets embrace crypto.

Expansion of Real-Time Payments

Real-time payments (RTP) are transactions that are processed instantly, providing immediate availability of funds. The adoption of RTP systems is growing globally, driven by consumer demand for speed and efficiency.

Faster Payment Systems: Countries like the United States, with systems like **Zelle** and **The Clearing House RTP**, and the United Kingdom, with the **Faster Payments Service**, are leading the way in RTP adoption. According to **Aite Group** (2021), real-time payments are expected to account for 20% of all electronic payments by 2025.

Business Applications: RTP is also gaining traction in business-to-business (B2B) transactions, where it can significantly improve cash flow management and operational efficiency. Companies are increasingly adopting RTP to streamline their financial operations and enhance customer satisfaction through quicker payment processing.

Rise of Biometric Authentication

Biometric authentication is becoming a standard security feature in digital payments, offering a higher level of security and convenience compared to traditional methods like passwords and PINs.

Fingerprint and Facial Recognition: Smartphones equipped with fingerprint scanners and facial recognition technology are enabling secure biometric authentication for digital payments. **Apple Pay**'s Face ID and **Samsung Pay**'s iris scanning are examples of how biometrics are enhancing payment security.

Behavioral Biometrics: The future may see the rise of behavioral biometrics, which analyze patterns in user behavior, such as typing speed and navigation habits, to authenticate transactions. This technology adds an additional layer of security by continuously monitoring user behavior to detect anomalies.

Increased Focus on Financial Inclusion

Digital payment platforms are playing a crucial role in enhancing financial inclusion by providing access to financial services for unbanked and underbanked populations.

Mobile Money Services: Services like **M-Pesa** in Kenya and **bKash** in Bangladesh have demonstrated the potential of mobile money to bring financial services to underserved regions. According to the **World Bank** (2020), there are over 1.7 billion unbanked adults globally, and mobile money services are crucial in reducing this number.

Government Initiatives: Governments and regulatory bodies are increasingly supporting digital payments to enhance financial inclusion. Initiatives like India's **Unified Payments Interface (UPI)** have transformed the digital payment landscape, making it easier for individuals and businesses to transact electronically.

Predictions for the Future of Digital Payments

Mainstream Adoption of Cryptocurrencies

Cryptocurrencies are expected to become more integrated into mainstream financial systems, with digital payments playing a pivotal role in this transition.

Central Bank Digital Currencies (CBDCs): Many central banks are exploring the development of digital currencies. CBDCs are digital versions of a country's fiat currency and are expected to coexist with traditional forms of money. According to a survey by the **Bank for International Settlements** (2021), 86% of central banks are actively researching CBDCs.

Retail and Institutional Use: Both retail consumers and institutional investors are showing increasing interest in cryptocurrencies. Digital wallets and payment platforms that support crypto transactions will become essential tools for managing these assets. The integration of cryptocurrencies into everyday transactions will further normalize their use.

Artificial Intelligence and Machine Learning

Artificial intelligence (AI) and machine learning (ML) will continue to transform digital payments by enhancing security, personalizing user experiences, and optimizing transaction processing.

Fraud Detection and Prevention: AI and ML algorithms can analyze transaction patterns in real-time to detect and prevent fraudulent activities. Platforms like **PayPal** and **Square** are already using these technologies to enhance their security measures.

Personalized Financial Services: AI-driven personalization will allow digital payment platforms to offer tailored financial advice, product recommendations, and customized user experiences. This level of personalization will improve user satisfaction and loyalty.

Internet of Things (IoT) Integration

The integration of digital payments with IoT devices is set to expand, enabling seamless and automated transactions in various contexts.

Smart Homes and Wearables: IoT devices, such as smart refrigerators that reorder groceries and wearable devices that make contactless payments, will become more prevalent. According to **Gartner** (2021), there will be over 25 billion IoT devices by 2025, many of which will have payment capabilities.

Automated Payments: IoT will enable automated payments for services like tolls, parking, and fuel. These automated systems will enhance convenience and efficiency, reducing the need for manual intervention in everyday transactions.

Strengthening Data Privacy and Security

As digital payments become more widespread, the focus on

data privacy and security will intensify. Ensuring the protection of user data will be paramount for gaining and maintaining consumer trust.

Enhanced Encryption: The development of more advanced encryption technologies will protect data in transit and at rest, making it more difficult for cybercriminals to access sensitive information.

Regulatory Compliance: Compliance with data protection regulations, such as the General Data Protection Regulation (GDPR) in Europe and the California Consumer Privacy Act (CCPA) in the United States, will be crucial. Payment platforms will need to ensure that their data handling practices meet these stringent standards.

Generations Alpha and Z are redefining consumer behavior and reshaping markets across the globe. Born into a digital-first world, these cohorts are influencing trends in technology, sustainability, and brand interaction, compelling companies to adapt to their unique preferences and demands. This section explores the distinct characteristics of Gen Alpha and Gen Z, their impact on various industries, and how businesses are responding to these emerging market forces.

Characteristics of Gen Alpha and Gen Z

Gen Alpha

Generation Alpha, born from 2010 onwards, is growing up in an environment dominated by advanced technology and digital connectivity. This generation is characterized by its:

- **Technological Proficiency**: From an early age, Gen Alpha interacts with smart devices, AI, and other advanced technologies, making them the most digitally literate generation yet.

- **Influence on Family Spending**: Despite their young age, Gen Alpha has significant sway over family purchasing decisions, particularly in categories like technology, entertainment, and food.
- **Educational Expectations**: With access to online learning platforms and digital resources, Gen Alpha expects personalized and engaging educational experiences.

Gen Z

Generation Z, born between 1997 and 2012, is the first cohort of true digital natives. Key traits include:

- **Social Media Savvy**: Gen Z spends a considerable amount of time on social media platforms like TikTok, Instagram, and Snapchat, using these channels for communication, entertainment, and shopping.
- **Value-Driven Consumption**: This generation prioritizes sustainability, diversity, and social justice, favoring brands that align with their values.
- **Entrepreneurial Spirit**: Many Gen Z individuals aspire to be entrepreneurs, leveraging digital tools and platforms to create and market their own products or services.

Impact on Technology and Media

Embrace of Emerging Technologies

Both generations are enthusiastic adopters of emerging technologies. Their comfort with digital interfaces and quick adoption of new gadgets drive demand for innovative products.

- **Augmented Reality (AR) and Virtual Reality (VR)**: Gen Z and Alpha are significant drivers of AR and VR technologies,

utilizing these tools for gaming, social media, and education. According to **Statista** (2021), the AR market is expected to grow from $6.21 billion in 2020 to $198 billion by 2025, driven largely by young users.
- **AI and Personalization**: These generations expect highly personalized digital experiences. AI-driven recommendations on platforms like Netflix and Spotify cater to their preferences, setting a standard for personalization across industries.

Influence on Social Media and Content Consumption

Social media is a central part of daily life for Gen Z and Alpha, shaping their content consumption habits and expectations.

- **Short-Form Content**: Platforms like TikTok and Instagram Reels thrive on short, engaging content. A report by **Business Insider** (2020) highlights that 60% of Gen Z TikTok users create their own content, indicating high engagement levels.
- **Influencer Marketing**: Influencers play a crucial role in shaping the opinions and purchasing decisions of these generations. Brands are increasingly collaborating with influencers to reach younger audiences authentically.

Impact on Retail and E-Commerce

Rise of Social Commerce

Gen Z and Alpha are pioneers of social commerce, blending social media and shopping into a seamless experience.

- **Instagram Shopping and TikTok Marketplace**: These platforms allow users to discover and purchase products directly from social media. According to **eMarketer** (2021), social commerce sales in the US are expected to reach $36.09 billion by 2023, driven by young consumers.

Preference for Sustainable and Ethical Brands

Sustainability and ethics are paramount for Gen Z and Alpha, influencing their purchasing decisions significantly.

- **Eco-Friendly Products**: Brands offering sustainable products or those with transparent supply chains are favored by these consumers. A survey by **First Insight** (2020) found that 62% of Gen Z prefers to buy from sustainable brands.
- **Corporate Social Responsibility (CSR)**: Companies that actively engage in social and environmental causes resonate well with these generations. They expect brands to take a stand on important issues and contribute positively to society.

Impact on Financial Services

Digital-First Banking

Gen Z and Alpha's preference for digital solutions extends to their banking habits.

- **Mobile Banking and Fintech**: Traditional banking is being challenged by fintech innovations. Apps like **Chime**, **Robinhood**, and **Venmo** cater to the needs of these tech-savvy users with features like fee-free banking, investing, and instant money transfers. According to **J.D. Power** (2020), 52% of Gen Z uses mobile banking apps as their primary banking method.
- **Cryptocurrencies and Blockchain**: Younger generations are

more open to cryptocurrencies as part of their investment portfolios. A report by **Gemini** (2021) revealed that nearly 63% of Gen Z view cryptocurrencies as the future of finance.

Impact on Education and Learning
E-Learning and Digital Education Tools
Gen Alpha and Gen Z have revolutionized the educational sector by embracing digital learning tools.

- **Online Learning Platforms**: Services like **Khan Academy**, **Coursera**, and **Duolingo** are popular among these generations for supplementary learning. The COVID-19 pandemic accelerated the adoption of these platforms, a trend that is likely to continue. According to **EdTech Magazine** (2020), the e-learning market is expected to reach $325 billion by 2025.
- **Gamified Learning**: Platforms incorporating gamification, like **Quizlet** and **Kahoot!**, engage students through interactive and enjoyable learning experiences. This approach caters to their preference for dynamic and interactive content.

Business Strategies to Engage Gen Alpha and Gen Z
Leveraging Technology and Innovation
Businesses need to continuously innovate to meet the high expectations of these tech-savvy generations.

- **Adopting AR and VR**: Brands are integrating AR and VR into their marketing and customer engagement strategies. For example, **IKEA's** AR app allows users to visualize furniture in their homes, enhancing the shopping experience.

- **Enhancing Personalization**: Using AI to provide personalized experiences, from product recommendations to marketing messages, helps capture and retain the attention of Gen Z and Alpha.

Emphasizing Sustainability and Ethics

To appeal to the value-driven Gen Z and Alpha, companies must prioritize sustainability and ethical practices.

- **Transparent Communication**: Clear communication about sustainable practices and CSR efforts builds trust and loyalty. Brands like **Patagonia** and **TOMS** are successful examples of companies that have integrated these values into their core operations.
- **Inclusive Marketing**: Representation and inclusivity in marketing campaigns resonate strongly with these generations. Brands need to showcase diversity and inclusivity to connect with their audience authentically.

Engaging Through Social Media and Influencers

Harnessing the power of social media and influencers is crucial for reaching these generations.

- **Collaborations with Influencers**: Partnering with micro and macro-influencers can amplify brand messages and increase engagement. Influencers provide authenticity and relatability, making them effective in driving brand loyalty.
- **Interactive and Engaging Content**: Creating content that encourages interaction, such as polls, challenges, and user-generated content, can boost engagement and foster a sense of community.

Potential Innovations and Technological Advancements in Digital Payments

The digital payments landscape is constantly evolving, driven by rapid technological advancements and changing consumer behaviors. Innovations in this space not only enhance the convenience and security of financial transactions but also have the potential to reshape the global financial ecosystem. This section explores some of the most promising innovations and technological advancements in digital payments.

1. Blockchain and Cryptocurrencies

Decentralized Finance (DeFi)

Blockchain technology is at the forefront of financial innovation, with cryptocurrencies like Bitcoin and Ethereum leading the charge. Decentralized finance, or DeFi, leverages blockchain to create a more open and transparent financial system. DeFi platforms offer services such as lending, borrowing, and trading without traditional intermediaries like banks.

Smart Contracts: These self-executing contracts with the terms directly written into code automate transactions and reduce the need for intermediaries. Smart contracts are crucial in DeFi applications, ensuring transparency and security.

Central Bank Digital Currencies (CBDCs)

Governments around the world are exploring the development of Central Bank Digital Currencies (CBDCs). These digital currencies aim to combine the benefits of cryptocurrencies with the stability of traditional fiat currencies. CBDCs could streamline payment systems, reduce transaction costs, and enhance financial inclusion.

China's Digital Yuan: China is leading the way with its digital yuan, which has undergone extensive testing and implementation. The digital yuan aims to increase financial inclusion and reduce the costs associated with cash transactions.

2. Artificial Intelligence and Machine Learning

Fraud Detection and Prevention

Artificial intelligence (AI) and machine learning (ML) are revolutionizing fraud detection and prevention in digital payments. These technologies analyze vast amounts of transaction data to identify patterns and detect anomalies that may indicate fraudulent activity.

Real-time Analysis: AI algorithms can monitor transactions in real-time, flagging suspicious activities and preventing fraud before it occurs. This capability significantly enhances the security of digital payments.

Personalized Financial Services

AI and ML also enable personalized financial services by analyzing user behavior and preferences. Digital payment platforms can offer tailored financial advice, personalized offers, and customized user experiences.

Chatbots and Virtual Assistants: AI-powered chatbots and virtual assistants provide instant customer support and financial guidance, enhancing user experience and satisfaction. These tools can handle routine inquiries and provide personalized financial recommendations.

3. Biometric Authentication

Enhanced Security Measures

Biometric authentication methods, such as fingerprint scanning, facial recognition, and iris scanning, provide an additional layer of security for digital payments. These methods are more secure than traditional passwords and PINs, reducing the risk of unauthorized access.

Facial Recognition: Platforms like Apple Pay use Face ID technology to authenticate transactions, ensuring that only the authorized user can initiate payments. This method is quick, convenient, and highly secure.

Behavioral Biometrics

Behavioral biometrics analyze patterns in user behavior, such as typing speed and navigation habits, to authenticate transactions. This technology continuously monitors user behavior to detect anomalies and enhance security.

Continuous Authentication: Behavioral biometrics provide continuous authentication, making it difficult for fraudsters to replicate user behavior and gain unauthorized access.

4. Internet of Things (IoT)

Connected Devices

The integration of digital payments with IoT devices is set to expand, enabling seamless and automated transactions across various contexts. IoT devices, such as smart refrigerators and wearable devices, can facilitate automatic payments for services like groceries and utilities.

Wearable Payments: Smartwatches and fitness trackers with payment capabilities allow users to make contactless payments quickly and conveniently. Brands like Apple, Garmin, and Samsung are leading the way in wearable payments.

Smart Contracts in IoT

Smart contracts integrated with IoT devices can automate transactions and enforce agreements without the need for intermediaries. This innovation has the potential to streamline processes and reduce transaction costs in various industries.

Supply Chain Management: Smart contracts can automate payments and enforce terms in supply chain transactions, improving efficiency and transparency.

5. Augmented Reality (AR) and Virtual Reality (VR)

Enhanced Shopping Experiences

AR and VR technologies are transforming the shopping experience, allowing consumers to visualize products and make payments in immersive environments. These technologies provide interactive and engaging experiences, driving consumer engagement and satisfaction.

Virtual Try-Ons: Retailers are using AR to offer virtual try-ons, allowing customers to see how products like clothing and accessories will look before making a purchase. This innovation reduces return rates and enhances the shopping experience.

Virtual Stores and Showrooms

VR enables the creation of virtual stores and showrooms, where customers can explore products and make purchases in a virtual environment. This technology offers a unique and immersive shopping experience, attracting tech-savvy consumers.

Virtual Real Estate Tours: The real estate industry is using VR to offer virtual property tours, allowing potential buyers to explore properties remotely and make secure payments.

6. Real-Time Payments and Open Banking

Instant Transactions

Real-time payment systems enable instant fund transfers, providing immediate availability of funds. This innovation enhances the efficiency and convenience of financial transactions, benefiting both consumers and businesses.

Faster Payments: Systems like The Clearing House RTP and Zelle in the United States offer real-time payments, reducing the waiting time for funds to clear and improving cash flow management.

Open Banking

Open banking initiatives allow third-party developers to build applications and services around financial institutions. By using open APIs, open banking enhances transparency, competition, and innovation in the financial sector.

API Integration: Open banking APIs enable seamless integration between banks and fintech companies, offering consumers more choices and better financial services. This collaboration fosters innovation and improves customer experience.

7. Enhanced Privacy and Data Protection

Data Encryption and Tokenization

Advanced data encryption and tokenization techniques protect sensitive information during transactions. These technologies ensure that personal and financial data is secure and reduce the risk of data breaches.

End-to-End Encryption: Platforms like Apple Pay and Google Pay use end-to-end encryption to protect data throughout the transaction process, ensuring that sensitive information remains secure.

Privacy-Enhancing Technologies

Privacy-enhancing technologies, such as zero-knowledge proofs and homomorphic encryption, allow data to be processed without revealing sensitive information. These innovations enhance privacy and security in digital payments.

Zero-Knowledge Proofs: This technology enables one party to prove to another that a statement is true without revealing any additional information. Zero-knowledge proofs can enhance privacy in financial transactions by protecting sensitive data.

Chapter 9

Chapter 8: Global Perspectives

Adoption of Digital Wallets and Payment Apps Worldwide

Digital wallets and payment apps have dramatically reshaped the global financial landscape, offering unparalleled convenience, security, and efficiency in monetary transactions. The adoption of these technologies has surged worldwide, driven by technological advancements, evolving consumer behaviors, and supportive regulatory frameworks. This section explores the global adoption of digital wallets and payment apps, highlighting key trends and developments across different regions.

North America

In North America, digital wallets and payment apps have seen substantial growth, propelled by the region's advanced technological infrastructure and high smartphone penetration rates.

United States: Digital wallets such as **Apple Pay**, **Google Pay**, and **Samsung Pay** are widely used for both online and in-store purchases. According to a report by **Statista** (2021), mobile payment transactions in the U.S. are projected to exceed $700 billion by 2023. The convenience of contactless payments, particularly during the COVID-19 pandemic, has accelerated adoption. Many retailers and service providers now offer contactless payment options, making digital wallets more integrated into everyday life. Furthermore, the integration of digital wallets with loyalty programs and discounts has incentivized consumers to switch from traditional payment methods.

Canada: Similarly, Canada has witnessed increased usage of digital wallets. Interac, a Canadian interbank network, reported a significant rise in mobile payment transactions, with over 61% of Canadians using digital payment methods in 2020. Canadian banks and fintech companies have been proactive in promoting digital wallets through various campaigns and partnerships, enhancing consumer trust and adoption. The support from major financial institutions has been pivotal in driving the usage of digital payment solutions.

Europe

Europe has been a pioneer in the adoption of digital payment technologies, supported by a robust regulatory framework and innovative fintech ecosystem.

United Kingdom: The UK leads the way in digital payment adoption, driven by the widespread use of contactless payments and mobile banking apps. The UK Finance report (2020) highlighted that contactless payments accounted for 27% of all payments in the UK in 2019. The UK's Open Banking initiative, which mandates banks to open their payment services and data to third-party providers, has spurred innovation and competition in the digital payments market. This regulatory support has encouraged the development of new payment solutions and increased consumer trust in digital transactions.

Nordic Countries: Sweden, Norway, Denmark, and Finland are at the forefront of digital payment adoption. Sweden aims to become a cashless society by 2023, with Swish, a mobile payment app, being widely used for peer-to-peer transfers and purchases. The Nordic countries' strong technological infrastructure, high internet penetration, and consumer trust in digital services have facilitated the rapid adoption of digital wallets. Government initiatives promoting digital payments and the decline in cash usage have further accelerated this trend.

Asia-Pacific

The Asia-Pacific region is experiencing explosive growth in digital wallet adoption, fueled by high smartphone penetration and a large unbanked population.

China: China is a global leader in digital payments, with Alipay and WeChat Pay dominating the market. According to the **People's Bank of China** (2020), digital payments accounted for over 83% of all transactions in 2020. The integration of digital wallets into everyday life, from shopping to utility payments, has driven widespread adoption. Chinese consumers prefer mobile payments for their convenience, speed, and integration with social media and e-commerce platforms. The government's support for digital payments and the rapid growth of the e-commerce sector have further fueled this adoption.

India: India's digital payment ecosystem has grown rapidly, supported by government initiatives like Digital India and the Unified Payments Interface (UPI). Apps like Paytm, PhonePe, and Google Pay are widely used for transactions, with UPI recording over 2 billion transactions monthly as of 2021. The government's push for a cashless economy, coupled with the high penetration of smartphones, has driven the adoption of digital wallets. UPI's interoperability and seamless user experience have made it a preferred payment method among consumers and merchants alike.

Africa

In Africa, digital wallets and mobile money services have significantly improved financial inclusion, providing access to financial services for the unbanked population.

Kenya: M-Pesa, launched by Safaricom, is a mobile money service that has revolutionized financial transactions in Kenya. With over 30 million users, M-Pesa enables money transfers, bill payments, and microloans, significantly enhancing financial inclusion. The success of M-Pesa has demonstrated the potential of mobile money services to provide financial access to underserved populations. Its widespread adoption has been driven by its ease of use, affordability, and extensive agent network.

Nigeria: Nigeria has also seen a rise in digital wallet adoption, with services like Paga and OPay gaining popularity. These platforms offer convenient and secure payment solutions, addressing the needs of the unbanked population. The growth of mobile money services in Nigeria is driven by the need for accessible financial services, the high mobile phone penetration, and the government's support for financial inclusion initiatives.

Latin America

Latin America is witnessing a rapid adoption of digital payment solutions, driven by a young population, increasing internet penetration, and a growing fintech sector.

Brazil: Brazil's digital payment landscape has been transformed by the introduction of Pix, an instant payment system developed by the Central Bank of Brazil. Launched in 2020,

CHAPTER 9

Pix enables real-time transactions and has quickly become a popular payment method, with millions of users adopting the service within its first year. The system's ease of use, coupled with its widespread acceptance by merchants and financial institutions, has driven its rapid adoption.

Mexico: In Mexico, digital wallets like MercadoPago and Clip are gaining traction, providing secure and convenient payment options for consumers and businesses. The Mexican government's initiatives to promote financial inclusion and the rise of e-commerce have further accelerated the adoption of digital payment solutions.

Middle East

The Middle East is also seeing a rise in the adoption of digital wallets and payment apps, driven by a tech-savvy population and supportive government policies.

United Arab Emirates: The UAE is at the forefront of digital payment adoption in the Middle East. With a high smartphone penetration rate and a young, tech-savvy population, digital wallets like **Apple Pay**, **Google Pay**, and **Samsung Pay** are widely used. The UAE government's push for a digital economy and initiatives like Dubai's Smart City project have further supported the growth of digital payments.

Saudi Arabia: In Saudi Arabia, digital wallets like STC Pay and Mada Pay are becoming increasingly popular. The Saudi government's Vision 2030 plan, which aims to diversify the economy and promote digital transformation, has played a crucial role in driving the adoption of digital payment solutions.

Factors Driving Adoption

Several factors contribute to the widespread adoption of digital wallets and payment apps worldwide:

Technological Advancements

The proliferation of smartphones and advancements in mobile technology have made digital wallets more accessible and user-friendly. High-speed internet connectivity and improved cyber-security measures have further boosted consumer confidence in using these platforms.

Changing Consumer Behaviors

Consumers' preference for convenience and speed in financial transactions has driven the adoption of digital wallets. The COVID-19 pandemic accelerated this shift, as contactless payments became essential for reducing physical contact.

Regulatory Support

Supportive regulatory frameworks and government initiatives have played a crucial role in promoting digital payment adoption. For instance, the European Union's Payment Services Directive (PSD2) has fostered innovation and competition in the payment services market.

Financial Inclusion

In regions with large unbanked populations, digital wallets provide an entry point to financial services. Mobile money services, particularly in Africa and Asia, have significantly improved financial inclusion by offering accessible and affordable financial solutions.

CHAPTER 9

Case Studies from Different Countries on Digital Wallets and Payment Apps

Digital wallets and payment apps have revolutionized financial transactions across the globe. However, the adoption and impact of these technologies vary significantly from one country to another. This section explores case studies from China, Kenya, Sweden, and India, highlighting the unique factors driving adoption and the impact on their respective financial ecosystems.

China: Alipay and WeChat Pay

China stands out as a global leader in digital payments, with Alipay and WeChat Pay dominating the market. These platforms have become integral to daily life, facilitating a wide range of transactions from shopping to bill payments.

Alipay

Alipay, launched by Alibaba Group, is one of the most popular digital wallets in China. It offers a comprehensive suite of financial services, including payments, investments, and insurance. Alipay's widespread adoption can be attributed to its seamless integration with Alibaba's e-commerce platforms and extensive network of partner merchants.

Impact: Alipay has significantly reduced the reliance on cash, with over 1.3 billion users worldwide as of 2021. The platform's success has driven financial inclusion, providing access to financial services for millions of unbanked individuals. Alipay also supports China's ambitious plans for a cashless society, enhancing the efficiency and security of financial transactions.

WeChat Pay

WeChat Pay, a subsidiary of Tencent, leverages the popularity of the WeChat messaging app to facilitate digital payments.

Integrated within the WeChat ecosystem, WeChat Pay allows users to send money, pay bills, and make purchases with ease.

Impact: With over 900 million active users, WeChat Pay has transformed the payment landscape in China. Its integration with various services, including ride-hailing and food delivery, has made it indispensable for daily transactions. WeChat Pay's success illustrates the potential of integrating financial services within social media platforms, creating a seamless user experience.

Kenya: M-Pesa

Kenya's M-Pesa is a pioneering mobile money service that has revolutionized financial transactions in the country. Launched by Safaricom in 2007, M-Pesa allows users to store, send, and receive money using their mobile phones.

M-Pesa

M-Pesa's success lies in its ability to provide financial services to the unbanked population. With over 30 million users, M-Pesa facilitates money transfers, bill payments, and microloans, significantly enhancing financial inclusion.

Impact: M-Pesa has had a profound impact on Kenya's economy, enabling financial access for millions of people. A study by the **World Bank** (2018) found that M-Pesa has lifted 2% of Kenyan households out of poverty by providing them with a secure and convenient way to manage their finances. M-Pesa's model has been replicated in other countries, highlighting its potential to address financial exclusion globally.

Sweden: Swish

Sweden is leading the way towards becoming a cashless society, with digital payments dominating the financial landscape. Swish, a mobile payment app, is a key player in this transformation.

Swish

Launched in 2012 by major Swedish banks, Swish allows real-time transfers between bank accounts using mobile phones. It is widely used for peer-to-peer payments, online shopping, and even charity donations.

Impact: Swish has over 7.8 million users in a country of 10 million, demonstrating its widespread adoption. Its success is attributed to the high level of trust in banks and technology, as well as the convenience of instant payments. Swish has played a crucial role in Sweden's move towards a cashless society, reducing the need for physical cash and enhancing the efficiency of financial transactions.

India: UPI and Paytm

India's digital payment ecosystem has grown rapidly, driven by government initiatives and innovative fintech solutions. The Unified Payments Interface (UPI) and Paytm are at the forefront of this transformation.

Unified Payments Interface (UPI)

UPI, launched by the National Payments Corporation of India (NPCI) in 2016, is a real-time payment system that enables instant money transfers between bank accounts. UPI's open architecture allows integration with various banking and fintech apps, promoting widespread adoption.

Impact: UPI recorded over 2 billion transactions monthly as of 2021, highlighting its significant impact on India's payment landscape. The platform has enhanced financial inclusion by providing a simple and secure way to transact digitally. UPI's interoperability and seamless user experience have made it a preferred payment method among consumers and merchants alike.

Paytm

Paytm, one of India's leading digital wallets, offers a wide range of services, including payments, banking, and investments. Its user-friendly interface and extensive merchant network have driven its popularity.

Impact: Paytm has over 350 million users, making it one of the most widely used digital wallets in India. The platform has played a crucial role in promoting digital payments, particularly among small merchants and rural populations. Paytm's success underscores the importance of user-friendly interfaces and extensive merchant networks in driving the adoption of digital payment solutions.

Factors Driving Adoption

Several factors contribute to the widespread adoption of digital wallets and payment apps in these countries:

Technological Advancements

The proliferation of smartphones and advancements in mobile technology have made digital wallets more accessible and user-friendly. High-speed internet connectivity and improved cybersecurity measures have further boosted consumer confidence in using these platforms.

Changing Consumer Behaviors

Consumers' preference for convenience and speed in financial transactions has driven the adoption of digital wallets. The COVID-19 pandemic accelerated this shift, as contactless payments became essential for reducing physical contact.

Regulatory Support

Supportive regulatory frameworks and government initiatives have played a crucial role in promoting digital payment adoption. For instance, the European Union's Payment Services Directive

(PSD2) has fostered innovation and competition in the payment services market.

Financial Inclusion

In regions with large unbanked populations, digital wallets provide an entry point to financial services. Mobile money services, particularly in Africa and Asia, have significantly improved financial inclusion by offering accessible and affordable financial solutions.

Cultural and Economic Factors Influencing the Usage of Digital Wallets and Payment Apps

Digital wallets and payment apps have rapidly gained popularity across the globe, but their adoption and usage vary significantly from one region to another. Cultural and economic factors play a crucial role in shaping how these technologies are embraced by different populations. This section delves into the cultural and economic factors that influence the usage of digital wallets and payment apps, with examples from various countries.

Cultural Factors

Trust in Technology

Trust in technology and financial institutions is a significant cultural factor influencing the adoption of digital wallets. In countries where there is high trust in digital solutions and financial institutions, the adoption rate of digital wallets is generally higher.

China: In China, there is a high level of trust in technology due to the strong presence of tech giants like Alibaba and Tencent. This trust has facilitated the widespread adoption of Alipay and WeChat Pay. The integration of these payment platforms into everyday activities, such as shopping, commuting, and dining, has made them indispensable to Chinese consumers.

Nordic Countries: Countries like Sweden and Denmark exhibit high levels of trust in technology and digital solutions. This trust extends to digital banking and payment systems, contributing to the widespread use of digital wallets like Swish. The high trust in financial institutions and regulatory frameworks also supports the adoption of digital payments.

Social Norms and Behavior

Social norms and behaviors significantly impact the adoption of digital wallets. In societies where there is a strong social influence and a trend towards digitalization, people are more likely to adopt new technologies.

India: In India, the social norm of following trends and the influence of social networks have contributed to the rapid adoption of digital wallets like Paytm and PhonePe. Government initiatives promoting digital payments have also played a role in shaping social behaviors towards cashless transactions.

Kenya: In Kenya, mobile money services like M-Pesa have become a social norm, particularly in urban areas. The convenience and security offered by M-Pesa have made it a preferred payment method for many Kenyans, influencing social behaviors towards digital transactions.

Cultural Attitudes Towards Privacy

Cultural attitudes towards privacy can affect the adoption of digital wallets. In regions where people are more concerned about privacy and data security, the adoption of digital payment solutions may be slower.

United States: In the United States, privacy concerns are more pronounced, and people are often wary of sharing their financial information online. This has led to a slower adoption rate of digital wallets compared to countries like China, where privacy concerns are less of a barrier.

European Union: The European Union has stringent data protection regulations, such as the General Data Protection Regulation (GDPR). While these regulations ensure high levels of data protection, they also require digital wallet providers to comply with rigorous standards, which can influence the adoption rate.

Economic Factors

Financial Inclusion

Financial inclusion is a critical economic factor influencing the adoption of digital wallets. In regions with large unbanked populations, digital wallets provide an entry point to financial services, driving adoption.

Sub-Saharan Africa: In Sub-Saharan Africa, mobile money services like M-Pesa in Kenya and MTN Mobile Money in Ghana have significantly improved financial inclusion. These services offer basic financial services to people who do not have access to traditional banking, facilitating economic participation and growth.

Southeast Asia: In countries like Indonesia and the Philippines, digital wallets such as GCash and OVO have helped improve financial inclusion by providing accessible financial services to the unbanked population. These platforms enable users to perform transactions, save money, and access credit, contributing to economic development.

Economic Stability

Economic stability and growth can influence the adoption of digital wallets. In stable economies with growing disposable incomes, people are more likely to adopt new financial technologies.

South Korea: South Korea's strong economy and technological advancement have led to high adoption rates of digital wallets like KakaoPay and Naver Pay. The country's economic stability has allowed consumers to embrace these technologies for their convenience and efficiency.

Japan: Despite being a technologically advanced country, Japan has a lower adoption rate of digital wallets compared to South Korea. This can be attributed to the country's long-standing preference for cash transactions and a conservative approach towards new financial technologies.

Government Policies and Initiatives

Government policies and initiatives play a crucial role in promoting the adoption of digital wallets. Supportive policies and incentives can encourage people to switch to digital payment methods.

India: The Indian government's Digital India initiative and the demonetization drive in 2016 significantly boosted the adoption of digital wallets. By promoting a cashless economy and incentivizing digital transactions, the government has encouraged both consumers and businesses to embrace digital payment solutions.

European Union: The EU's Payment Services Directive (PSD2) aims to increase competition and innovation in the payment services market. By allowing third-party providers to access bank account information with customer consent, PSD2 has facilitated the development and adoption of digital wallets and payment apps across *Europe*.

Technological Infrastructure

The availability and quality of technological infrastructure, such as internet connectivity and smartphone penetration, are crucial economic factors influencing the adoption of digital wallets.

China: China's advanced technological infrastructure, including widespread internet access and high smartphone penetration, has facilitated the rapid adoption of digital wallets. The integration of payment apps with e-commerce platforms and social media has further boosted their usage.

Nigeria: In Nigeria, the growth of mobile money services has been driven by the increasing availability of mobile phones and improving internet connectivity. However, challenges such as inconsistent network coverage and high data costs still pose barriers to widespread adoption.

Market Competition

The level of competition among digital wallet providers can influence adoption rates. In highly competitive markets, providers are incentivized to offer better services and incentives to attract users.

United States: In the U.S., the competition among digital wallet providers like Apple Pay, Google Pay, and PayPal has led to the development of innovative features and promotional offers to attract users. This competitive environment drives adoption by providing consumers with a variety of options and benefits.

India: India's digital wallet market is highly competitive, with players like Paytm, PhonePe, and Google Pay vying for market share. The intense competition has led to frequent cashback offers, discounts, and partnerships with merchants, driving the adoption of digital wallets.

Chapter 10

Challenges and Opportunities

Digital wallets and payment apps offer numerous benefits, including convenience, security, and efficiency. Despite their advantages, various barriers hinder their widespread adoption. Addressing these barriers with effective solutions is crucial for enhancing the adoption of digital payment technologies globally. This section explores the primary barriers to adoption and potential solutions.

Barriers to Adoption

Lack of Trust in Digital Payment Systems

One of the significant barriers to adopting digital wallets and payment apps is the lack of trust among consumers. Concerns about security, data privacy, and the potential for fraud deter many people from using these technologies.

Security Concerns: Consumers worry about the safety of their financial information when using digital payment systems. High-profile data breaches and cyberattacks have heightened these concerns.

Data Privacy: The collection and use of personal data by digital payment platforms raise privacy issues. Consumers are often unaware of how their data is being used or fear that it might be misused.

Limited Access to Technology

Access to the necessary technology is another barrier to adoption. In many regions, particularly in developing countries, limited internet connectivity and low smartphone penetration rates restrict the use of digital wallets.

Internet Connectivity: Reliable internet access is essential for digital payments. In areas with poor connectivity, consumers cannot use digital wallets effectively.

Smartphone Penetration: Digital wallets typically require smartphones. In regions where smartphones are not widely available or affordable, adoption rates are low.

Regulatory and Legal Challenges

Regulatory and legal frameworks can either facilitate or hinder the adoption of digital wallets. In some countries, stringent regulations and lack of clear legal guidelines pose significant challenges.

Regulatory Uncertainty: Ambiguous or constantly changing regulations create uncertainty for both providers and users of digital payment systems. This uncertainty can deter investment and innovation.

Compliance Costs: Meeting regulatory requirements can be costly for digital wallet providers, particularly smaller fintech companies. High compliance costs can limit the availability and expansion of these services.

Consumer Habits and Cultural Resistance

Long-standing consumer habits and cultural resistance to

change can impede the adoption of digital wallets. People who are accustomed to cash or traditional banking methods may be reluctant to switch to digital payments.

Preference for Cash: In many cultures, cash is still the preferred method of transaction due to its tangibility and widespread acceptance. Convincing consumers to switch from cash to digital payments requires significant effort.

Digital Literacy: A lack of digital literacy can also be a barrier. Consumers who are not comfortable using digital technologies may be hesitant to adopt digital wallets.

Potential Solutions

Enhancing Security and Building Trust

Building trust is essential for increasing the adoption of digital wallets. Implementing robust security measures and transparent data practices can help address consumer concerns.

Advanced Security Measures: Digital wallet providers should implement advanced security features such as biometric authentication, encryption, and tokenization to protect user data. Educating consumers about these measures can help build trust.

Transparent Data Practices: Providers should be transparent about how they collect, use, and protect consumer data. Clear privacy policies and regular updates on data security practices can reassure users.

Improving Access to Technology

Increasing access to the necessary technology is crucial for expanding the use of digital wallets, particularly in underserved regions.

Expanding Internet Connectivity: Governments and private companies should invest in improving internet infrastructure to ensure reliable connectivity in all regions. Public-private partnerships can be effective in achieving this goal.

Affordable Smartphones: Providing affordable smartphones through subsidies or financing options can help increase smartphone penetration. Programs that recycle or refurbish old smartphones can also make them more accessible.

Streamlining Regulatory Frameworks

Creating clear and supportive regulatory frameworks can facilitate the adoption of digital wallets and encourage innovation.

Consistent Regulations: Governments should work towards creating consistent and predictable regulatory environments for digital payments. Clear guidelines and streamlined processes can reduce uncertainty for providers and users.

Supporting Innovation: Regulators should balance oversight with support for innovation. Sandboxing and pilot programs can allow new technologies to be tested in a controlled environment, fostering innovation while ensuring consumer protection.

Promoting Digital Literacy and Cultural Change

Promoting digital literacy and encouraging cultural acceptance of digital payments can drive adoption.

Education and Training: Educational campaigns and training programs can help increase digital literacy. These initiatives should target all age groups and demographics to ensure widespread understanding and comfort with digital technologies.

Incentives and Rewards: Offering incentives such as discounts, cashback, or rewards for using digital wallets can encourage consumers to make the switch. These incentives can help overcome initial resistance and create positive experiences with digital payments.

Collaborating with Traditional Financial Institutions

Collaborating with traditional financial institutions can help bridge the gap between conventional banking and digital payments.

Bank Partnerships: Digital wallet providers can partner with banks to offer integrated services. Such collaborations can leverage the trust and reach of traditional banks while providing the innovation and convenience of digital wallets.

Co-branded Solutions: Offering co-branded digital wallet solutions that combine the strengths of both traditional banks and fintech companies can attract a broader user base. These solutions can provide seamless transitions for users accustomed to traditional banking.

Case Studies

China: China's success with digital wallets like Alipay and WeChat Pay illustrates the importance of trust and technology access. The high trust in technology companies, widespread smartphone usage, and strong regulatory support have driven the rapid adoption of digital payments.

Kenya: M-Pesa's success in Kenya highlights the role of financial inclusion and cultural adaptation. By providing accessible financial services to the unbanked and integrating with everyday activities, M-Pesa has become an essential part of the Kenyan financial ecosystem.

Sweden: Sweden's journey towards a cashless society demonstrates the impact of cultural change and government support. Swish, a popular mobile payment app, has gained widespread acceptance due to its convenience and the cultural shift towards digital transactions.

India: India's rapid adoption of digital payments, driven by government initiatives like Digital India and the Unified Payments Interface (UPI), shows the effectiveness of regulatory support and incentives. Collaborations between fintech companies and traditional banks have further accelerated adoption.

CHAPTER 10

Opportunities for Businesses and Financial Institutions in Digital Wallets and Payment Apps

The rise of digital wallets and payment apps has created a wealth of opportunities for businesses and financial institutions. These technologies offer a range of benefits, including improved customer experience, enhanced operational efficiency, and access to new revenue streams. This section explores the key opportunities that digital wallets and payment apps present to businesses and financial institutions.

Enhanced Customer Experience

Convenience and Speed

Digital wallets and payment apps provide unparalleled convenience and speed in financial transactions. Customers can make payments with just a few taps on their smartphones, avoiding the need for cash or physical cards. This seamless experience is highly valued in today's fast-paced world.

Contactless Payments: The adoption of contactless payments has surged, particularly during the COVID-19 pandemic. Businesses that offer digital payment options can cater to the growing demand for touch-free transactions, enhancing customer satisfaction and loyalty.

Integration with Loyalty Programs: Digital wallets can integrate with loyalty programs, making it easier for customers to earn and redeem rewards. This integration encourages repeat business and enhances customer engagement.

Personalization

Digital payment platforms can leverage data analytics to offer personalized experiences to customers. By analyzing transaction data, businesses can gain insights into customer preferences and behavior, enabling them to tailor offers and promotions.

Targeted Marketing: Businesses can use insights from digital wallets to create targeted marketing campaigns. Personalized offers and promotions based on customer spending habits can increase conversion rates and drive sales.

Customer Insights: Detailed transaction data provides valuable insights into customer behavior. Businesses can use this information to improve products, services, and customer interactions, leading to higher satisfaction and retention.

Operational Efficiency

Streamlined Processes

Digital wallets and payment apps streamline various business processes, reducing the time and effort required for transactions and administrative tasks.

Automated Payments: Businesses can automate recurring payments, such as subscriptions and bills, using digital wallets. This automation reduces manual intervention, minimizes errors, and ensures timely payments.

Inventory Management: Integration with digital payment systems allows for real-time tracking of sales and inventory levels. Businesses can optimize inventory management, reducing stockouts and overstock situations.

Cost Savings

By adopting digital payment solutions, businesses can achieve significant cost savings in several areas.

Reduced Cash Handling: Handling cash involves costs related to security, storage, and transportation. Digital payments reduce the reliance on cash, leading to lower operational costs.

Lower Transaction Fees: Digital wallets often have lower transaction fees compared to traditional payment methods, especially for small and medium-sized enterprises (SMEs).

These savings can improve profit margins.

Access to New Revenue Streams

Financial Services

Digital wallets open up opportunities for businesses to offer a range of financial services, creating new revenue streams.

Microloans and Credit: Businesses can offer microloans and credit facilities through digital wallets. By leveraging transaction data and advanced algorithms, they can assess creditworthiness and provide tailored financial products to customers.

Investment Services: Digital payment platforms can provide investment services, such as micro-investing and robo-advisory. These services attract users looking to grow their wealth, generating additional revenue for businesses.

Merchant Services

Digital wallets can offer a variety of merchant services, helping businesses expand their offerings and attract more customers.

Payment Processing: Businesses can act as payment processors for other merchants, earning fees for facilitating transactions. This service is particularly beneficial for e-commerce platforms and marketplaces.

Point-of-Sale Solutions: Providing point-of-sale (POS) solutions integrated with digital wallets can attract small businesses and retailers. These solutions simplify transactions and offer additional features like sales analytics and inventory management.

Financial Inclusion

Expanding Customer Base

Digital wallets provide access to financial services for the unbanked and underbanked populations, enabling businesses to reach new customer segments.

Emerging Markets: In many emerging markets, a significant portion of the population lacks access to traditional banking services. Digital wallets can bridge this gap, allowing businesses to tap into these underserved markets.

Inclusive Financial Products: By offering inclusive financial products, such as low-cost remittances and savings accounts, businesses can attract a broader customer base. This inclusivity not only drives growth but also contributes to social and economic development.

Government Partnerships

Businesses and financial institutions can collaborate with governments to promote financial inclusion through digital wallets.

Subsidy Distribution: Governments can use digital wallets to distribute subsidies and welfare payments efficiently. Businesses involved in these initiatives can benefit from increased transaction volumes and improved brand reputation.

Public Services: Partnering with governments to provide digital payment solutions for public services, such as utility payments and transportation, can enhance financial inclusion and create new business opportunities.

Innovation and Competitive Advantage

Staying Ahead of the Curve

Adopting digital wallets and payment apps allows businesses to stay ahead of the competition by embracing innovation and technology.

Early Adoption: Early adopters of digital payment technologies can differentiate themselves from competitors and attract tech-savvy customers. This competitive edge can lead to increased market share and brand loyalty.

Continuous Improvement: By continuously innovating and improving digital payment solutions, businesses can maintain their competitive advantage. Investing in research and development ensures that they stay at the forefront of technological advancements.

Ecosystem Development

Businesses can develop ecosystems around digital wallets, creating interconnected services that enhance user experience and drive growth.

Partnerships and Collaborations: Forming partnerships with other businesses, fintech companies, and financial institutions can expand the capabilities of digital wallets. Collaborations can lead to the development of new features and services, attracting more users.

Platform Ecosystem: Creating a platform ecosystem where multiple services, such as payments, banking, and e-commerce, are integrated into a single digital wallet can enhance user convenience and loyalty. This ecosystem approach fosters a comprehensive digital experience.

The Role of Government and Regulation in the Adoption of Digital Wallets and Payment Apps

Governments and regulatory bodies play a critical role in shaping the landscape of digital wallets and payment apps. Through supportive policies, regulatory frameworks, and initiatives aimed at promoting financial inclusion and security, governments can significantly influence the adoption and success of digital payment technologies. This section explores the various roles of government and regulation in this context, highlighting key examples and potential impacts.

Promoting Financial Inclusion

Policies and Initiatives

Governments can promote financial inclusion by creating policies and initiatives that support the use of digital wallets and payment apps, especially in underserved populations.

India's Digital India Initiative: The Indian government's Digital India initiative aims to transform India into a digitally empowered society. A significant component of this initiative is promoting digital payments through the Unified Payments Interface (UPI), which has revolutionized the payment landscape by making digital transactions accessible and affordable for millions.

Kenya's Mobile Money Framework: The Kenyan government has supported mobile money services like M-Pesa, which have drastically increased financial inclusion. By creating a conducive regulatory environment and encouraging innovation, the government has enabled millions of previously unbanked individuals to access financial services.

Subsidies and Incentives

Governments can provide subsidies and incentives to encourage the use of digital wallets and payment apps among the population.

Subsidy Distribution through Digital Wallets: Some governments use digital wallets to distribute subsidies and welfare payments efficiently. For example, India uses digital wallets and bank accounts to transfer subsidies directly to beneficiaries, reducing leakage and ensuring timely payments.

Tax Incentives: Offering tax incentives to businesses that adopt digital payment solutions can encourage widespread usage. These incentives can reduce the cost burden on businesses, making it more attractive to switch from cash-based to digital transactions.

Ensuring Security and Consumer Protection

Regulatory Frameworks

Establishing robust regulatory frameworks is essential to ensure the security and protection of consumers using digital payment systems.

Europe's PSD2 Directive: The European Union's Payment Services Directive 2 (PSD2) aims to increase competition and innovation in the payment services market while ensuring high levels of consumer protection. PSD2 mandates strong customer authentication (SCA) and opens up bank APIs to third-party providers, fostering a secure and competitive environment for digital payments.

The General Data Protection Regulation (GDPR): GDPR, also in the EU, sets stringent guidelines for data protection and privacy. For digital wallet providers, compliance with GDPR ensures that consumers' personal and financial data are adequately protected, building trust and confidence in digital payment systems.

Fraud Prevention and Security Standards

Governments and regulatory bodies can set security standards and requirements to prevent fraud and protect consumers.

PCI DSS Compliance: The Payment Card Industry Data Security Standard (PCI DSS) is a set of security standards designed to ensure that all companies that process, store, or transmit credit card information maintain a secure environment. Governments can mandate compliance with PCI DSS for digital wallet providers to enhance security.

Regulatory Sandboxes: Establishing regulatory sandboxes allows fintech companies to test new digital payment solutions in a controlled environment. This approach enables regulators to monitor developments and ensure that new technologies meet security and compliance standards before full-scale implementation.

Fostering Innovation and Competition

Open Banking

Open banking initiatives can foster innovation and competition by requiring banks to share customer data with third-party providers, subject to customer consent.

UK's Open Banking Initiative: The UK's Open Banking initiative mandates that banks open their payment services and data to third-party providers. This has led to a surge in fintech innovation, with new digital wallets and payment apps offering enhanced services and better customer experiences.

Australia's Consumer Data Right (CDR): Similar to the UK's Open Banking initiative, Australia's CDR allows consumers to control their data and share it with accredited third-party providers. This empowers consumers and promotes competition among financial service providers.

Support for Fintech Ecosystems

Governments can support the development of fintech ecosystems through grants, funding, and infrastructure development.

Singapore's Fintech Festival: Singapore hosts the annual Fintech Festival, which brings together industry leaders, startups, and regulators to discuss and promote fintech innovations. The government's active support for fintech through such events and funding initiatives has made Singapore a global fintech hub.

Fintech Hubs and Incubators: Establishing fintech hubs and incubators can provide startups with the resources and support they need to develop innovative digital payment solutions. These hubs can offer mentorship, funding, and collaboration opportunities with established financial institutions.

Addressing Barriers to Adoption

Education and Awareness Campaigns

Governments can run education and awareness campaigns to inform the public about the benefits and security of digital wallets and payment apps.

Public Awareness Programs: Governments can collaborate with financial institutions and fintech companies to run public awareness programs that educate citizens about digital payments. These programs can address common concerns about security and privacy, encouraging more people to adopt digital wallets.

Digital Literacy Initiatives: Enhancing digital literacy through targeted programs can help individuals understand and use digital payment technologies effectively. These initiatives are particularly important in rural and underserved areas.

Infrastructure Development

Investing in the necessary infrastructure to support digital payments is crucial for widespread adoption.

Improving Internet Connectivity: Governments can invest in improving internet connectivity, particularly in rural and remote areas. Reliable internet access is essential for the effective use of digital wallets and payment apps.

Promoting Smartphone Penetration: Providing subsidies or financing options for smartphones can increase their penetration, enabling more people to access digital payment solutions.

Case Studies

India: India's success with UPI and the Digital India initiative highlights the importance of government support and regulatory frameworks in promoting digital payments. By encouraging innovation and ensuring security, the government has facilitated the rapid adoption of digital wallets.

European Union: The EU's PSD2 and GDPR regulations demonstrate how robust regulatory frameworks can foster innovation while ensuring consumer protection. These regulations have created a secure and competitive environment for digital payments.

Kenya: Kenya's support for mobile money services like M-Pesa showcases the impact of government policies on financial inclusion. By creating a conducive regulatory environment, the government has enabled millions to access financial services.

11

Chapter 11

The adoption and impact of digital wallets and payment apps have been substantial across various regions worldwide. Key findings from the analysis of barriers to adoption, opportunities for businesses and financial institutions, and the role of government and regulation provide valuable insights into the dynamics of this evolving financial technology landscape.

One of the foremost barriers to adoption is the lack of trust among consumers. Concerns about security, data privacy, and the potential for fraud deter many from using these technologies. High-profile data breaches and cyberattacks have heightened these fears, leading to reluctance in adopting digital wallets. Additionally, consumers are often unaware of how their data is being used or fear it might be misused, further contributing to their hesitancy.

Solution: Building trust through robust security measures such as biometric authentication, encryption, and tokenization is essential. Providers must also be transparent about their data practices, educating consumers about how their information is protected and used.

Limited Access to Technology

Access to necessary technology is another barrier, especially in developing regions. Limited internet connectivity and low smartphone penetration rates restrict the use of digital wallets.

Solution: Improving internet infrastructure and making smartphones more affordable through subsidies or financing options can help increase adoption. Public-private partnerships can be instrumental in enhancing technological access.

Regulatory and Legal Challenges

Regulatory and legal frameworks can either facilitate or hinder the adoption of digital wallets. In some countries, stringent regulations and lack of clear legal guidelines pose significant challenges.

Solution: Governments should aim to create consistent and predictable regulatory environments. Clear guidelines and streamlined processes can reduce uncertainty for providers and users, fostering a more conducive environment for digital payments.

Consumer Habits and Cultural Resistance

Long-standing consumer habits and cultural resistance to change also impede the adoption of digital wallets. In many cultures, cash remains the preferred method of transaction due to its tangibility and widespread acceptance. Furthermore, a lack of digital literacy can hinder the adoption of these technologies.

Solution: Educational campaigns and training programs that enhance digital literacy and inform the public about the benefits of digital payments can help overcome these barriers. Incentives such as discounts and rewards can also encourage consumers to adopt digital wallets.

Opportunities for Businesses and Financial Institutions

Digital wallets and payment apps present numerous opportunities for businesses and financial institutions, enabling them to enhance customer experience, improve operational efficiency, and access new revenue streams:

Enhanced Customer Experience

Digital wallets offer unparalleled convenience and speed in financial transactions. Customers can make payments with just a few taps on their smartphones, avoiding the need for cash or physical cards. This seamless experience is highly valued in today's fast-paced world. Additionally, the integration of digital wallets with loyalty programs can enhance customer engagement and encourage repeat business.

Solution: Businesses can leverage data analytics to offer personalized experiences, creating targeted marketing campaigns and improving customer interactions based on insights from transaction data.

Operational Efficiency

Digital wallets streamline various business processes, reducing the time and effort required for transactions and administrative tasks. Automated payments, real-time tracking of sales and inventory levels, and reduced cash handling can lead to significant cost savings and improved operational efficiency.

Solution: Businesses should adopt digital payment solutions that integrate with their existing systems, enabling seamless transactions and efficient management of operations.

Access to New Revenue Streams

Digital wallets open up opportunities for businesses to offer a range of financial services, such as microloans, credit facilities, and investment services. Additionally, providing merchant services like payment processing and point-of-sale solutions can attract more customers and generate additional revenue.

Solution: Businesses and financial institutions should explore partnerships and collaborations to expand their offerings and create new revenue streams through digital wallets.

Financial Inclusion

Digital wallets provide access to financial services for the unbanked and underbanked populations, enabling businesses to reach new customer segments. By offering inclusive financial products and partnering with governments to promote financial inclusion, businesses can drive growth and contribute to social and economic development.

Solution: Focus on developing inclusive financial products and collaborating with governments on initiatives that promote financial inclusion through digital wallets.

Innovation and Competitive Advantage

Adopting digital wallets and payment apps allows businesses to stay ahead of the competition by embracing innovation and technology. Early adoption of digital payment technologies can differentiate businesses from competitors and attract tech-savvy customers.

Solution: Continuous innovation and improvement of digital payment solutions are essential. Businesses should invest in research and development to stay at the forefront of technological advancements and maintain their competitive edge.

The Role of Government and Regulation

Governments and regulatory bodies play a pivotal role in the adoption and success of digital wallets and payment apps:

Promoting Financial Inclusion

Governments can promote financial inclusion by creating policies and initiatives that support the use of digital wallets, particularly in underserved populations. Subsidies and incentives can encourage the adoption of digital payment solutions, while partnerships with businesses can enhance the distribution of financial services.

Solution: Implement policies and initiatives that promote digital payments and provide incentives for businesses and consumers to adopt these technologies.

Ensuring Security and Consumer Protection

Establishing robust regulatory frameworks is essential to ensure the security and protection of consumers using digital payment systems. Regulations like Europe's PSD2 and GDPR set high standards for security and data protection, fostering a secure environment for digital payments.

Solution: Governments should establish and enforce security standards and regulations that protect consumers while encouraging innovation in the digital payment sector.

Fostering Innovation and Competition

Open banking initiatives and support for fintech ecosystems can foster innovation and competition in the digital payment market. By requiring banks to share customer data with third-party providers and supporting fintech development through grants and infrastructure, governments can create a vibrant and competitive digital payment ecosystem.

Solution: Promote open banking initiatives and support the development of fintech ecosystems through funding, infrastructure development, and regulatory sandboxes.

Addressing Barriers to Adoption

Governments can address barriers to adoption through education and awareness campaigns, improving internet connectivity, and promoting smartphone penetration. Collaborating with businesses and financial institutions on these initiatives can enhance the uptake of digital payment technologies.

Solution: Implement educational campaigns, invest in infrastructure development, and provide subsidies for smartphones to increase access to digital payment technologies.

Implications for the Future of Finance: Digital Wallets and Payment Apps

The rapid adoption of digital wallets and payment apps is fundamentally transforming the financial landscape. These technologies are not only changing how people manage and spend their money but are also influencing broader financial systems and institutions. As digital wallets and payment apps continue to evolve, they are likely to have far-reaching implications for the future of finance. This section explores these implications in terms of financial inclusion, consumer behavior, banking, regulatory landscapes, and technological innovation.

Financial Inclusion

Bridging the Gap for the Unbanked

One of the most significant impacts of digital wallets and payment apps is their potential to enhance financial inclusion. In many developing countries, large portions of the population remain unbanked or underbanked, lacking access to traditional banking services. Digital wallets offer a way to bridge this gap by providing a convenient and accessible platform for financial transactions.

Case Study: M-Pesa in Kenya: M-Pesa has revolutionized financial inclusion in Kenya by allowing millions of unbanked individuals to perform financial transactions using their mobile phones. The success of M-Pesa demonstrates the potential for digital wallets to bring financial services to underserved populations, fostering economic participation and growth.

Government Initiatives

Governments can leverage digital wallets to efficiently distribute subsidies and social welfare payments, ensuring that financial aid reaches the intended recipients without leakage or delay. This approach not only promotes financial inclusion but also enhances transparency and reduces corruption.

India's Direct Benefit Transfer (DBT): The Indian government's DBT program uses digital wallets and bank accounts to transfer subsidies directly to beneficiaries. This method has significantly reduced administrative costs and improved the efficiency of welfare distribution.

Changing Consumer Behavior

Convenience and Speed

Digital wallets and payment apps offer unparalleled convenience and speed, influencing consumer behavior and expectations. Consumers increasingly prefer the ease of making transactions with a few taps on their smartphones, leading to a decline in the use of cash and physical cards.

Contactless Payments: The COVID-19 pandemic has accelerated the shift towards contactless payments, as consumers seek safer and more hygienic payment methods. The increased adoption of contactless payments is likely to persist, further reducing reliance on cash.

Integration with Other Services

Digital wallets are becoming comprehensive financial tools that integrate various services, including payments, budgeting, investments, and loyalty programs. This integration enhances the user experience and encourages consumers to adopt digital wallets as their primary financial management tool.

Super Apps: Platforms like WeChat in China have evolved into super apps, offering a wide range of services beyond payments, such as social networking, e-commerce, and ride-hailing. The success of super apps illustrates the potential for digital wallets to become central hubs for managing various aspects of consumers' financial lives.

Transforming Banking and Financial Services

Disintermediation

The rise of digital wallets and payment apps is leading to disintermediation in the financial sector, where traditional intermediaries such as banks are bypassed in favor of direct peer-to-peer transactions.

Peer-to-Peer Payments: Platforms like Venmo and Cash App enable users to transfer money directly to each other without the need for a bank as an intermediary. This trend challenges traditional banking models and prompts banks to innovate and adapt.

Collaboration and Competition

While digital wallets pose a competitive threat to traditional banks, they also present opportunities for collaboration. Banks can partner with fintech companies to offer enhanced digital payment solutions and leverage their technological expertise.

Open Banking: Initiatives like open banking, where banks share customer data with third-party providers (with customer consent), foster collaboration between traditional financial institutions and fintech companies. This collaboration can lead to innovative products and services that enhance customer experience and drive growth.

Regulatory and Security Challenges

Evolving Regulatory Landscapes

The rapid growth of digital wallets and payment apps necessitates evolving regulatory frameworks to ensure security, consumer protection, and fair competition. Regulators must balance the need for innovation with the need for oversight.

PSD2 in Europe: The Payment Services Directive 2 (PSD2) in the European Union aims to increase competition and innovation while ensuring high levels of security and consumer protection. PSD2 mandates strong customer authentication (SCA) and open APIs, setting a benchmark for other regions to follow.

Enhancing Security Measures

As digital payments become more prevalent, ensuring the security of transactions and protecting consumer data are paramount. Providers must implement robust security measures to prevent fraud and cyberattacks.

Biometric Authentication: The use of biometric authentication, such as fingerprint scanning and facial recognition, enhances the security of digital wallets. These technologies provide an additional layer of protection and build consumer trust.

Tokenization: Tokenization replaces sensitive payment information with unique tokens during transactions, reducing the risk of data breaches. This technology is becoming a standard practice for securing digital payments.

Technological Innovation

Blockchain and Cryptocurrencies

Blockchain technology and cryptocurrencies are poised to further disrupt the financial landscape. Digital wallets are increasingly integrating cryptocurrency transactions, providing users with more options for managing their assets.

Central Bank Digital Currencies (CBDCs): Many central banks are exploring the development of CBDCs, which could coexist with traditional fiat currencies. CBDCs aim to combine the benefits of cryptocurrencies with the stability of government-backed currencies, potentially revolutionizing digital payments.

Decentralized Finance (DeFi): DeFi platforms use blockchain technology to offer financial services without traditional intermediaries. Digital wallets that support DeFi can provide users with access to lending, borrowing, and trading services, fostering a more open and decentralized financial system.

Artificial Intelligence and Machine Learning

Artificial intelligence (AI) and machine learning (ML) are transforming digital payments by enhancing security, personalizing user experiences, and optimizing transaction processes.

Fraud Detection and Prevention: AI and ML algorithms can analyze transaction patterns in real-time to detect and prevent fraudulent activities. This capability significantly enhances the security of digital payments.

Personalized Financial Services: AI-driven personalization allows digital payment platforms to offer tailored financial advice, product recommendations, and customized user experiences. This level of personalization improves user satisfaction and loyalty.

Final Thoughts on the Impact of Gen Alpha and Gen Z on Cashless Transactions

The emergence of Generation Alpha and Generation Z as influential consumer groups is accelerating the shift toward cashless transactions. These generations, characterized by their digital nativity and tech-savviness, are driving the adoption of digital wallets and payment apps, reshaping the financial landscape in profound ways. Understanding their impact on cashless transactions provides insights into the future of finance and commerce.

CHAPTER 11

Digital Natives Redefining Payments

Gen Z, born between the mid-1990s and early 2010s, and Gen Alpha, born from 2010 onwards, have grown up in an era dominated by digital technology. Their comfort with smartphones, social media, and the internet translates into a natural inclination towards digital payment methods.

Mobile Payments as the Norm: For these generations, using mobile payment apps like Apple Pay, Google Pay, Venmo, and Cash App is second nature. The convenience of making transactions with a tap or a scan aligns with their preference for efficiency and speed.

Integration with Social Media: Payment features integrated within social media platforms (e.g., Facebook Pay, Instagram Shopping) cater to the habits of Gen Z and Gen Alpha, who spend a significant amount of time on these platforms. This seamless integration blurs the lines between socializing and shopping, further embedding cashless transactions into their daily lives.

Shifting Consumer Expectations

Gen Z and Gen Alpha's expectations for seamless and instantaneous transactions are pushing businesses and financial institutions to innovate continuously. They demand not only speed but also security, personalization, and an engaging user experience.

Enhanced Security Features: These generations are aware of cybersecurity threats and expect robust security measures. Biometric authentication, end-to-end encryption, and real-time fraud monitoring are critical features that meet their security expectations.

Personalized Experiences: AI-driven personalization in payment apps can offer tailored financial advice, spending insights, and customized rewards, resonating with Gen Z and Gen Alpha's desire for individualized experiences.

Impact on Financial Institutions and Services

The rise of Gen Z and Gen Alpha is prompting traditional financial institutions to adapt to the changing landscape. Banks and financial services are increasingly integrating digital payment solutions to stay relevant.

Digital-First Banking: Neobanks and digital-first banking services are particularly appealing to these generations. Platforms like Chime, Revolut, and Monzo offer user-friendly interfaces, low fees, and features tailored to young consumers' needs.

Cryptocurrency and Decentralized Finance: Gen Z and Gen Alpha show a growing interest in cryptocurrencies and decentralized finance (DeFi). Digital wallets that support cryptocurrency transactions and DeFi services are becoming more popular, reflecting their openness to innovative financial products.

Influencing the Retail Landscape

Retailers are also evolving to cater to the preferences of these digitally native consumers. The demand for seamless, cashless transactions is driving the adoption of various payment technologies.

Contactless Payments: The COVID-19 pandemic accelerated the adoption of contactless payments, a trend that aligns with the preferences of Gen Z and Gen Alpha. Retailers are now more likely to offer contactless payment options to meet consumer demand for hygiene and convenience.

Omnichannel Shopping: These generations expect a seamless shopping experience across online and offline channels. Retailers are integrating digital payment options into their e-commerce platforms and physical stores, ensuring a cohesive and convenient customer journey.

Promoting Financial Inclusion

Gen Z and Gen Alpha's embrace of digital wallets and payment apps also has significant implications for financial inclusion. These technologies can provide access to financial services for unbanked and underbanked populations, particularly in developing regions.

Mobile Money Services: In regions like Sub-Saharan Africa and Southeast Asia, mobile money services such as M-Pesa and GCash are expanding financial access. These services allow users to perform transactions, save money, and access credit using their mobile phones.

Government Initiatives: Governments are leveraging digital payment technologies to promote financial inclusion. Initiatives that distribute subsidies and social welfare payments through digital wallets ensure that financial aid reaches those in need efficiently and transparently.

Driving Innovation and Future Trends

The influence of Gen Z and Gen Alpha extends beyond current trends to shape the future of digital payments. Their preferences and behaviors are driving continuous innovation in payment technologies.

Blockchain and Digital Currencies: Interest in blockchain technology and digital currencies among these generations is fostering the development of new financial products and services. Central bank digital currencies (CBDCs) and decentralized finance platforms are examples of innovations that could gain traction.

Super Apps: The concept of super apps, which integrate multiple services such as payments, messaging, and shopping, is likely to grow. Inspired by platforms like WeChat, super apps offer a comprehensive digital ecosystem that appeals to the all-in-one convenience sought by Gen Z and Gen Alpha.

The impact of Gen Z and Gen Alpha on cashless transactions is transformative. Their digital nativity and expectations for seamless, secure, and personalized experiences are driving the rapid adoption and evolution of digital wallets and payment apps. As these generations continue to mature and their purchasing power increases, their influence will only grow stronger, pushing businesses, financial institutions, and governments to innovate and adapt. Embracing the preferences and behaviors of Gen Z and Gen Alpha is not just a trend but a necessity for staying relevant in the future of finance. The move towards a cashless society, led by these digitally native generations, promises a future of greater financial inclusion, efficiency, and innovation.

12

Chapter 12

Appendices

- Glossary of terms

Apple Pay: A digital wallet and mobile payment service by Apple Inc. that allows users to make payments in person, in iOS apps, and on the web using Safari.

Banking Apps: Mobile applications provided by traditional banks that offer services such as balance checks, fund transfers, bill payments, and mobile deposits.

Blockchain: A decentralized digital ledger that records transactions across many computers in such a way that the registered transactions cannot be altered retroactively.

Cash App: A mobile payment service developed by Square, Inc. that allows users to transfer money to one another using a mobile phone app.

Closed Wallets: Digital wallets specific to a particular company that can only be used to transact with that company.

Coinbase: A digital currency wallet and platform where merchants and consumers can transact with new digital currencies like bitcoin, ethereum, and litecoin.

Cryptocurrency Wallets: Digital wallets that store cryptocurrencies and manage the cryptographic keys associated with digital currencies.

Cryptocurrency Payment Apps: Mobile applications that enable users to make transactions using their digital currency holdings.

Digital Divide: The gap between those who have easy access to the internet and technology, and those who do not.

Digital Fluency: The ability to effectively and critically navigate, evaluate, and create information using a range of digital technologies.

Digital Wallets: Also known as e-wallets, these are electronic devices or online services that allow individuals to make electronic transactions, storing users' payment information and passwords.

Experiential Economy: An economy where consumers prioritize experiences over material possessions.

Financial Literacy: The ability to understand and effectively use various financial skills, including personal financial management, budgeting, and investing.

Financially Literate: Having the knowledge and skills needed to make informed and effective decisions about financial resources.

Finfluencers: Financial influencers who share advice on budgeting, saving, investing, and using financial tools via social media platforms.

Gen Alpha: The generation born from 2013 onwards, growing up with advanced technology integrated into daily life.

Gen Z: The generation born between 1997 and 2012, characterized by their comfort with digital environments and technology.

Google Pay: A digital wallet and online payment system developed by Google to power in-app and tap-to-pay purchases on mobile devices.

Great Recession: The severe economic downturn that occurred worldwide from 2007 to 2009.

Internet of Things (IoT): A system of interrelated computing devices, mechanical and digital machines provided with unique identifiers, and the ability to transfer data over a network without requiring human-to-human or human-to-computer interaction.

Mobile Banking: A service provided by a bank or other financial institution that allows its customers to conduct financial transactions remotely using a mobile device.

Mobile Payment Apps: Mobile applications that facilitate in-store and online payments through mobile devices.

Open Wallets: Digital wallets that can be used for a wide range of transactions and are often issued by banks or institutions in collaboration with financial service providers.

PayPal: An online payments system that supports online money transfers and serves as an electronic alternative to traditional paper methods like checks and money orders.

Payment Apps: Mobile applications that facilitate the transfer of money between parties, often integrating with digital wallets for various financial activities.

Paytm: An Indian e-commerce payment system and financial technology company that offers digital wallets for payments at partner outlets.

Peer-to-Peer (P2P) Payment Apps: Mobile applications that allow users to transfer money directly to others using their mobile devices.

Retailer-Specific Apps: Mobile applications developed by individual retailers to enhance the shopping experience by integrating payment options, loyalty programs, and personalized offers.

Robinhood: A commission-free stock trading and investing app that offers users the ability to buy and sell stocks, ETFs, options, and cryptocurrencies.

Samsung Pay: A mobile payment and digital wallet service by Samsung Electronics that lets users make payments using compatible phones and other Samsung-produced devices.

Semi-Closed Wallets: Digital wallets that can be used at multiple locations but are limited to a specific list of merchants or vendors.

Socially Responsible Investing (SRI): An investment strategy which seeks to consider both financial return and social/environmental good to bring about a positive change.

Starbucks App: A mobile application by Starbucks that allows users to store funds and make purchases exclusively at Starbucks locations.

Venmo: A mobile payment service owned by PayPal that allows users to transfer money to one another using a mobile phone app.

Zelle: A United States-based digital payments network run by Early Warning Services that allows for peer-to-peer payments through a mobile app.

- Additional resources for further reading
- Survey results and data analysis

13

Chapter 13

References

Chapter 1 :

1. **Investopedia: What is a Digital Wallet?**

- Investopedia. (n.d.). What is a Digital Wallet? Retrieved from Investopedia

1. **NerdWallet: Best Mobile Payment Apps**

- NerdWallet. (n.d.). Best Mobile Payment Apps. Retrieved from NerdWallet

1. **TechCrunch: The Rise of Venmo**

- Constine, J. (2016, September 28). The Rise of Venmo: Explaining One of the Largest Consumer Product Acquisitions

Ever. Retrieved from TechCrunch

1. **CNBC: How Cash App Became Square's Big Moneymaker**

- McCullough, B. (2020, May 6). How Cash App Became Square's Big Moneymaker. Retrieved from CNBC

1. **Apple: About Apple Pay**

- Apple. (n.d.). Apple Pay. Retrieved from Apple

Gen Alpha and Gen Z Financial Behaviors

1. **McKinsey & Company: True Gen: Generation Z and its implications for companies**

- Francis, T., & Hoefel, F. (2018, November 12). 'True Gen': Generation Z and Its Implications for Companies. Retrieved from McKinsey & Company

1. **Deloitte: Understanding Generation Z in the Financial Services Industry**

- Deloitte. (n.d.). Understanding Generation Z in the Financial Services Industry. Retrieved from Deloitte

1. **Pew Research Center: Teens, Social Media & Technology**

- Pew Research Center. (2018, May 31). Teens, Social Media & Technology 2018. Retrieved from Pew Research Center

CHAPTER 13

1. **Forbes: How Social Media Influences Consumer Behavior**

- Forbes Agency Council. (2018, December 20). How Social Media Influences Consumer Behavior. Retrieved from Forbes

Security and Privacy Concerns

1. **Kaspersky: Digital Payment Security**

- Kaspersky. (n.d.). Digital Payment Security. Retrieved from Kaspersky

1. **Norton: Mobile Payment Security**

- Norton. (n.d.). Mobile Payment Security. Retrieved from Norton

1. **Consumer Reports: How to Make Your Digital Payments Secure**

- Consumer Reports. (2021, October 4). How to Make Your Digital Payments Secure. Retrieved from Consumer Reports

Financial Literacy and Digital Payments

1. **Visa: Financial Literacy Resources**

- Visa. (n.d.). Financial Literacy Resources. Retrieved from Visa

1. **OECD: Financial Literacy and Digitalization**

- OECD. (2018). Financial Literacy and Digitalisation: Policy Brief. Retrieved from OECD

1. **FINRA: Financial Literacy in the United States**

- FINRA Investor Education Foundation. (2016). Financial Capability in the United States 2016. Retrieved from FINRA

Future Trends in Cashless Transactions

1. **World Economic Forum: The Future of Payments**

- World Economic Forum. (2020, August 4). The Future of Payments Is Digital and Contactless. Retrieved from World Economic Forum

1. **Accenture: The Future of Digital Payments**

- Accenture. (2020). The Future of Digital Payments: Strategies for a Post-COVID World. Retrieved from Accenture

1. **McKinsey & Company: Global Payments Report**

- McKinsey & Company. (2020, October). The 2020 McKinsey Global Payments Report. Retrieved from McKinsey & Company

Global Perspectives

1. World Bank: Digital Financial Inclusion

- World Bank. (2018). Digital Financial Inclusion. Retrieved from World Bank

1. IMF: The Rise of Digital Money

- Adrian, T., & Mancini-Griffoli, T. (2019). The Rise of Digital Money. Retrieved from IMF

1. OECD: Digital Transformation in Financial Services

- OECD. (2020). Digital Disruption in Banking and its Impact on Competition. Retrieved from OECD

Challenges and Opportunities

1. Harvard Business Review: The Future of Cashless Payments

- Lal, R., & Sachdev, N. (2015, September). The Future of Cashless Payments. Retrieved from Harvard Business Review

1. PwC: Digital Banking and Financial Services

- PwC. (2020). The Future of Digital Banking. Retrieved from PwC

1. **Capgemini: World Payments Report**

- Capgemini. (2020). World Payments Report 2020. Retrieved from Capgemini
-

Francis, T., & Hoefel, F. (2018, November 12). 'True Gen': Generation Z and Its Implications for Companies. McKinsey & Company. Retrieved from McKinsey & Company
Deloitte. (n.d.). Understanding Generation Z in the Financial Services Industry. Retrieved from Deloitte
Pew Research Center. (2018, May 31). Teens, Social Media & Technology 2018. Retrieved from Pew Research Center
Forbes Agency Council. (2018, December 20). How Social Media Influences Consumer Behavior. Retrieved from Forbes
OECD. (2020). Digital Disruption in Banking and its Impact on Competition. Retrieved from OECDBank of America. (2020, October). OK Zoomer: Gen Z Primer. Retrieved from Bank of America
National Endowment for Financial Education (NEFE). (2020). Financial Literacy and Knowledge Among Gen Z. Retrieved from NEFE
Pew Research Center. (2018, May 31). Teens, Social Media & Technology 2018. Retrieved from Pew Research Center
Deloitte. (n.d.). Understanding Generation Z in the Financial Services Industry. Retrieved from Deloitte
Francis, T., & Hoefel, F. (2018, November 12). 'True Gen': Generation Z and Its Implications for Companies. McKinsey & Company. Retrieved from McKinsey & Company
OECD. (2020). Digital Disruption in Banking and its Impact on Competition. Retrieved from OECD

CHAPTER 13

Accenture. (2020). The Future of Digital Payments: Strategies for a Post-COVID World. Retrieved from Accenture

World Economic Forum. (2020, August 4). The Future of Payments Is Digital and Contactless. Retrieved from World Economic Forum

Capgemini. (2020). World Payments Report 2020. Retrieved from Capgemini

PwC. (2020). The Future of Digital Banking. Retrieved from PwC

Bank of America. (2020, October). OK Zoomer: Gen Z Primer. Retrieved from Bank of America

National Endowment for Financial Education (NEFE). (2020). Financial Literacy and Knowledge Among Gen Z. Retrieved from NEFE

Pew Research Center. (2018, May 31). Teens, Social Media & Technology 2018. Retrieved from Pew Research Center

Deloitte. (n.d.). Understanding Generation Z in the Financial Services Industry. Retrieved from Deloitte

Francis, T., & Hoefel, F. (2018, November 12). 'True Gen': Generation Z and Its Implications for Companies. McKinsey & Company. Retrieved from McKinsey & Company

OECD. (2020). Digital Disruption in Banking and its Impact on Competition. Retrieved from OECD

Accenture. (2020). The Future of Digital Payments: Strategies for a Post-COVID World. Retrieved from Accenture

World Economic Forum. (2020, August 4). The Future of Payments Is Digital and Contactless. Retrieved from World Economic Forum

Capgemini. (2020). World Payments Report 2020. Retrieved from Capgemini

PwC. (2020). The Future of Digital Banking. Retrieved from

PwC

Chapter 2:

Investopedia. (n.d.). What is a Digital Wallet? Retrieved from Investopedia

NerdWallet. (n.d.). Best Mobile Payment Apps. Retrieved from NerdWallet

Constine, J. (2016, September 28). The Rise of Venmo: Explaining One of the Largest Consumer Product Acquisitions Ever. Retrieved from TechCrunch

McCullough, B. (2020, May 6). How Cash App Became Square's Big Moneymaker. Retrieved from CNBC

Apple. (n.d.). Apple Pay. Retrieved from Apple

Paytm. (n.d.). Paytm Wallet. Retrieved from Paytm

Coinbase. (n.d.). Cryptocurrency Wallets. Retrieved from Coinbase

Zelle. (n.d.). How Zelle Works. Retrieved from Zelle

Chase. (n.d.). Chase Mobile Banking. Retrieved from Chase

Amazon. (n.d.). Amazon Payments. Retrieved from Amazon

BitPay. (n.d.). Cryptocurrency Payment Gateway. Retrieved from BitPay

Bank of America. (2020, October). OK Zoomer: Gen Z Primer. Retrieved from Bank of America

Investopedia. (n.d.). What is a Digital Wallet? Retrieved from Investopedia

NerdWallet. (n.d.). Best Mobile Payment Apps. Retrieved from NerdWallet

Constine, J. (2016, September 28). The Rise of Venmo: Explaining One of the Largest Consumer Product Acquisitions Ever. Retrieved from TechCrunch

McCullough, B. (2020, May 6). How Cash App Became

CHAPTER 13

Square's Big Moneymaker. Retrieved from CNBC
   Apple. (n.d.). Apple Pay. Retrieved from Apple
   Paytm. (n.d.). Paytm Wallet. Retrieved from Paytm
   Coinbase. (n.d.). Cryptocurrency Wallets. Retrieved from Coinbase
   Zelle. (n.d.). How Zelle Works. Retrieved from Zelle
   Chase. (n.d.). Chase Mobile Banking. Retrieved from Chase
   Amazon. (n.d.). Amazon Payments. Retrieved from Amazon
   BitPay. (n.d.). Cryptocurrency Payment Gateway. Retrieved from BitPay
   Nakamoto, S. (2009). Bitcoin: A Peer-to-Peer Electronic Cash System. Retrieved from Bitcoin.org
   Western Union. (n.d.). History of Western Union. Retrieved from Western Union
   Bank of America. (2020, October). OK Zoomer: Gen Z Primer. Retrieved from Bank of America
   Francis, T., & Hoefel, F. (2018, November 12). 'True Gen': Generation Z and Its Implications for Companies. McKinsey & Company. Retrieved from McKinsey & Company
   Constine, J. (2016, September 28). The Rise of Venmo: Explaining One of the Largest Consumer Product Acquisitions Ever. Retrieved from TechCrunch
   McCullough, B. (2020, May 6). How Cash App Became Square's Big Moneymaker. Retrieved from CNBC
   Apple. (n.d.). Apple Pay. Retrieved from Apple
   Investopedia. (n.d.). What is a Digital Wallet? Retrieved from Investopedia
   NerdWallet. (n.d.). Best Mobile Payment Apps. Retrieved from NerdWallet
   Paytm. (n.d.). Paytm Wallet. Retrieved from Paytm
   Coinbase. (n.d.). Cryptocurrency Wallets. Retrieved from

Coinbase

Zelle. (n.d.). How Zelle Works. Retrieved from Zelle

Chase. (n.d.). Chase Mobile Banking. Retrieved from [Chase](https://www.chase.com/digital/mobile-b

Chapter 3:

Deloitte. (2020). The Deloitte Global Millennial Survey 2020. Retrieved from Deloitte

Center for Generational Kinetics. (2019). The State of Gen Z 2019. Retrieved from GenHQ

Morning Consult. (2020). The State of Workers in the Gig Economy. Retrieved from Morning Consult

Pew Research Center. (2018). Teens, Social Media & Technology 2018. Retrieved from Pew Research Center

Francis, T., & Hoefel, F. (2018). 'True Gen': Generation Z and its implications for companies. McKinsey & Company. Retrieved from McKinsey & Company

Twenge, J. M. (2017). iGen: Why Today's Super-Connected Kids Are Growing Up Less Rebellious, More Tolerant, Less Happy—and Completely Unprepared for Adulthood. Simon & Schuster.

Gartner. (2019). Market Guide for AI Startups. Retrieved from Gartner

Common Sense Media. (2020). The Common Sense Census: Media Use by Tweens and Teens. Retrieved from Common Sense Media

Pew Research Center. (2019). Teens, Social Media & Technology 2018. Retrieved from Pew Research Center

Javelin Strategy & Research. (2020). Mobile Wallet Use Surges Among Gen Z. Retrieved from Javelin Strategy

Business Insider Intelligence. (2019). Venmo and the rise of social payments. Retrieved from Business Insider

CHAPTER 13

Charles Schwab. (2020). Gen Z and Investing: New Faces of Wealth. Retrieved from Charles Schwab

Acorns. (2020). Acorns hits 8 million sign-ups as micro-investing takes off. Retrieved from Acorns

NerdWallet. (2019). How Gen Z Is Using Budgeting Apps to Manage Money. Retrieved from NerdWallet

Gemini. (2021). The State of U.S. Crypto Report. Retrieved from Gemini

Pew Research Center. (2021). Teens, Social Media & Technology 2021. Retrieved from Pew Research Center

Council for Economic Education. (2020). Survey of the States: Economic and Personal Finance Education in Our Nation's Schools. Retrieved from [Council for Economic Education](https://www.councilforeconed.org/p

Pew Research Center. (2018). Teens, Social Media & Technology 2018. Retrieved from Pew Research Center

Pew Research Center. (2019). Mobile Fact Sheet. Retrieved from Pew Research Center

Center for Generational Kinetics. (2019). The State of Gen Z 2019. Retrieved from GenHQ

Dell Technologies. (2019). Gen Z: The Future Has Arrived. Retrieved from Dell Technologies

Deloitte. (2020). The Deloitte Global Millennial Survey 2020. Retrieved from Deloitte

Nielsen. (2019). How to Reach Gen Z: Understanding the Next Generation of Digital Consumers. Retrieved from Nielsen

Business Insider Intelligence. (2019). Venmo and the rise of social payments. Retrieved from Business Insider

Acorns. (2020). Acorns hits 8 million sign-ups as micro-investing takes off. Retrieved from Acorns

Gemini. (2021). The State of U.S. Crypto Report. Retrieved

from Gemini

Common Sense Media. (2020). The Common Sense Census: Media Use by Tweens and Teens. Retrieved from Common Sense Media

Chapter 4 :

1. **Business Insider Intelligence**. (2019). Venmo and the rise of social payments. Retrieved from Business Insider
2. **CNBC**. (2020, May 6). How Cash App Became Square's Big Moneymaker. Retrieved from CNBC
3. **Apple**. (n.d.). Apple Pay. Retrieved from Apple
4. **TechCrunch**. (2020, September 21). Google Pay is quietly becoming a powerful mobile payments app in India. Retrieved from TechCrunch
5. **Investopedia**. (n.d.). What is a Digital Wallet? Retrieved from Investopedia
6. **Samsung**. (n.d.). Samsung Pay. Retrieved from Samsung

Business Insider Intelligence. (2019). Venmo and the rise of social payments. Retrieved from Business Insider

Javelin Strategy & Research. (2020). Mobile Wallet Use Surges Among Gen Z. Retrieved from Javelin Strategy

Statista. (2021). Number of Apple Pay users worldwide. Retrieved from Statista

TechCrunch. (2020, September 21). Google Pay is quietly becoming a powerful mobile payments app in India. Retrieved from TechCrunch

1. Statista. (2021). Number of active PayPal accounts worldwide. Retrieved from Statista

Chapter 5:

Mediakix. (2019). Influencer Marketing Survey. Retrieved from Mediakix

Hootsuite. (2020). Digital 2020: Global Digital Overview. Retrieved from Hootsuite

Nielsen. (2020). Nielsen Global Trust in Advertising Report. Retrieved from Nielsen

Sprout Social. (2020). Sprout Social Index: Edition XVI: Above and Beyond. Retrieved from Sprout Social

Nielsen. (2020). Nielsen Global Trust in Advertising Report. Retrieved from Nielsen

Business Insider Intelligence. (2019). Venmo and the rise of social payments. Retrieved from Business Insider

Javelin Strategy & Research. (2020). Mobile Wallet Use Surges Among Gen Z. Retrieved from Javelin Strategy

Statista. (2021). Number of active PayPal accounts worldwide. Retrieved from Statista

TechCrunch. (2020, September 21). Google Pay is quietly becoming a powerful mobile payments app in India. Retrieved from TechCrunch

Sprout Social. (2020). Sprout Social Index: Edition XVI: Above and Beyond. Retrieved from Sprout Social

Chapter 6

Pew Research Center. (2018). Teens, Social Media & Technology 2018. Retrieved from Pew Research Center

Statista. (2020). Preferred authentication methods of internet users worldwide. Retrieved from Statista

Microsoft. (2019). The Need for Multi-Factor Authentication. Retrieved from Microsoft

App Annie. (2021). State of Mobile 2021. Retrieved from App Annie

Pew Research Center. (2019). Americans and Privacy: Concerned, Confused, and Feeling Lack of Control Over Their Personal Information. Retrieved from Pew Research Center

Chapter 7

FINRA Investor Education Foundation. (2018). The State of U.S. Financial Capability: The 2018 National Financial Capability Study. Retrieved from FINRA

The National Endowment for Financial Education. (2019). Financial Education in the U.S. Retrieved from NEFE

Jump$tart Coalition. (2020). Financial Literacy for Students. Retrieved from Jump$tart

Council for Economic Education. (2020). Survey of the States: Economic and Personal Finance Education in Our Nation's Schools. Retrieved from Council for Economic Education

Consumer Financial Protection Bureau. (2019). The financial well-being of America. Retrieved from CFPB

National Financial Educators Council. (2020). Financial Literacy Teacher Training. Retrieved from NFEC

University of Wisconsin-Madison. (2019). The Impact of High School Financial Education on Financial Knowledge and Behavior. Retrieved from University of Wisconsin-Madison

T. Rowe Price. (2020). Parents, Kids & Money Survey. Retrieved from T. Rowe Price

Khan Academy. (n.d.). Personal Finance. Retrieved from Khan Academy

Junior Achievement USA. (n.d.). Programs. Retrieved from Junior Achievement

Khan Academy. (n.d.). Personal Finance. Retrieved from Khan Academy

FINRA Investor Education Foundation. (2018). The State of U.S. Financial Capability: The 2018 National Financial Capability

Study. Retrieved from FINRA

The National Endowment for Financial Education. (2019). Financial Education in the U.S. Retrieved from NEFE

Consumer Financial Protection Bureau. (2019). The financial well-being of America. Retrieved from CFPB

Jump$tart Coalition. (2020). Financial Literacy for Students. Retrieved from Jump$tart

Council for Economic Education. (2020). Survey of the States: Economic and Personal Finance Education in Our Nation's Schools. Retrieved from Council for Economic Education

T. Rowe Price. (2020). Parents, Kids & Money Survey. Retrieved from T. Rowe Price

App Annie. (2021). State of Mobile 2021. Retrieved from App Annie

Junior Achievement USA. (n.d.). Programs. Retrieved from Junior Achievement

National Financial Educators Council. (2020). Financial Literacy Teacher Training. Retrieved from NFEC

Statista. (2021). Mobile Payment Transactions in the United States. Retrieved from Statista

World Bank. (2018). Global Findex Database 2017: Measuring Financial Inclusion and the Fintech Revolution. Retrieved from World Bank

NerdWallet. (2020). Budgeting Apps and Tools. Retrieved from NerdWallet

The National Bureau of Economic Research. (2019). The Impact of Automated Savings Programs. Retrieved from NBER

Chapter 8

1. **How Gen Alpha and Gen Z Are Shaping the Market**

   1. **Statista**. (2021). Augmented Reality (AR) Market Size

Worldwide. Retrieved from Statista
2. **Business Insider**. (2020). The TikTok Generation: Gen Z Trends and Behaviors. Retrieved from Business Insider
3. **eMarketer**. (2021). Social Commerce Sales to Reach $36 Billion in 2023. Retrieved from eMarketer
4. **First Insight**. (2020). The State of Consumer Spending: Gen Z Shoppers Demand Sustainable Retail. Retrieved from First Insight
5. **J.D. Power**. (2020). 2020 U.S. Retail Banking Satisfaction Study. Retrieved from J.D. Power
6. **Gemini**. (2021). The State of U.S. Crypto Report. Retrieved from Gemini
7. **EdTech Magazine**. (2020). E-Learning Market Trends 2020-2025. Retrieved from EdTech Magazine
8. **World Bank**. (2020). Global Findex Database 2017: Measuring Financial Inclusion and the Fintech Revolution. Retrieved from World Bank

2. **Potential Innovations and Technological Advancements in Digital Payments**

1. **Juniper Research**. (2021). Contactless Payment Transactions to Exceed $6 Trillion Globally by 2024. Retrieved from Juniper Research
2. **Statista**. (2021). Number of Cryptocurrency Wallet Users Worldwide. Retrieved from Statista
3. **Aite Group**. (2021). Real-Time Payments to Account for 20% of All Electronic Payments by 2025. Retrieved from Aite Group
4. **Bank for International Settlements**. (2021). CBDCs: An Opportunity for the Monetary System. Retrieved from BIS

5. **World Bank**. (2020). Global Findex Database 2017: Measuring Financial Inclusion and the Fintech Revolution. Retrieved from World Bank
6. **Gartner**. (2021). IoT Devices to Surpass 25 Billion by 2025. Retrieved from Gartner

3. Impact of Digital Payments on Financial Habits and Understanding

1. **Statista**. (2021). Mobile Payment Transactions in the United States. Retrieved from Statista
2. **World Bank**. (2018). Global Findex Database 2017: Measuring Financial Inclusion and the Fintech Revolution. Retrieved from World Bank
3. **NerdWallet**. (2020). Budgeting Apps and Tools. Retrieved from NerdWallet
4. **The National Bureau of Economic Research**. (2019). The Impact of Automated Savings Programs. Retrieved from NBER
5. **Pew Research Center**. (2019). Americans and Privacy: Concerned, Confused, and Feeling Lack of Control Over Their Personal Information. Retrieved from Pew Research Center

Chapter 9
Adoption of Digital Wallets and Payment Apps Worldwide

1. Statista. (2021). Mobile Payment Transactions in the United States. Retrieved from Statista
2. UK Finance. (2020). UK Payment Markets 2020. Retrieved from UK Finance

3. People's Bank of China. (2020). 2020 PBC Annual Report. Retrieved from PBC
4. World Bank. (2020). Global Findex Database 2017: Measuring Financial Inclusion and the Fintech Revolution. Retrieved from World Bank

Case Studies from Different Countries on Digital Wallets and Payment Apps

1. World Bank. (2018). The Global Findex Database 2017: Measuring Financial Inclusion and the Fintech Revolution. Retrieved from World Bank
2. Statista. (2021). Mobile Payment Transactions in the United States. Retrieved from Statista
3. People's Bank of China. (2020). 2020 PBC Annual Report. Retrieved from PBC
4. UK Finance. (2020). UK Payment Markets 2020. Retrieved from UK Finance

Cultural and Economic Factors Influencing the Usage of Digital Wallets and Payment Apps

1. World Bank. (2018). The Global Findex Database 2017: Measuring Financial Inclusion and the Fintech Revolution. Retrieved from World Bank
2. People's Bank of China. (2020). 2020 PBC Annual Report. Retrieved from PBC
3. Statista. (2021). Mobile Payment Transactions in the United States. Retrieved from Statista
4. UK Finance. (2020). UK Payment Markets 2020. Retrieved from UK Finance

Chapter 10:

Barriers to Adoption and Potential Solutions

1. World Bank. (2018). Global Findex Database 2017: Measuring Financial Inclusion and the Fintech Revolution. Retrieved from World Bank
2. Kaspersky. (n.d.). Digital Payment Security. Retrieved from Kaspersky
3. Norton. (n.d.). Mobile Payment Security. Retrieved from Norton
4. OECD. (2020). Digital Disruption in Banking and its Impact on Competition. Retrieved from OECD
5. Pew Research Center. (2019). Americans and Privacy: Concerned, Confused, and Feeling Lack of Control Over Their Personal Information. Retrieved from Pew Research Center
6. Statista. (2021). Mobile Payment Transactions in the United States. Retrieved from Statista

Opportunities for Businesses and Financial Institutions

1. McKinsey & Company. (2020). Global Payments Report. Retrieved from McKinsey & Company
2. Accenture. (2020). The Future of Digital Payments: Strategies for a Post-COVID World. Retrieved from Accenture
3. Capgemini. (2020). World Payments Report 2020. Retrieved from Capgemini
4. PwC. (2020). The Future of Digital Banking. Retrieved from PwC
5. Gartner. (2019). Market Guide for AI Startups. Retrieved

from Gartner
6. Deloitte. (2020). The Deloitte Global Millennial Survey 2020. Retrieved from Deloitte

The Role of Government and Regulation

1. World Bank. (2018). Global Findex Database 2017: Measuring Financial Inclusion and the Fintech Revolution. Retrieved from World Bank
2. European Union. (2018). Payment Services Directive 2 (PSD2). Retrieved from European Union
3. General Data Protection Regulation (GDPR). (2018). Retrieved from GDPR
4. Reserve Bank of India. (2019). Guidelines for Prepaid Payment Instruments. Retrieved from RBI
5. Central Bank of Kenya. (2020). Mobile Money Services in Kenya. Retrieved from Central Bank of Kenya
6. UK Finance. (2020). UK Payment Markets 2020. Retrieved from UK Finance
7. Monetary Authority of Singapore. (2020). FinTech Regulatory Sandbox Guidelines. Retrieved from MAS

www.ingramcontent.com/pod-product-compliance
Lightning Source LLC
Chambersburg PA
CBHW071918210526
45479CB00002B/465